C000127053

THE
NORTH YORKSHIRE MOORS RAILWAY

·A PAST and PRESENT COMPANION·

THE RAILWAY.

Hail, Modern Science! who dares now to scan
The endless powers, that thou canst give to man?
Aided by thee, o'er trackless seas he glides,
Braves adverse winds, and stems opposing tides,
Earth's depths attains, her hidden wealth explores,
Applies to varied use her boundless stores;
On iron roads (o'er levell'd hills convey'd,
Through blasted rocks, or tunnell'd mountains made,)
By steam propell'd, pursues his rapid way,
And ends ere noon, what erst employ'd the day,
Air, water, fire, at STEPHENSON'S command,
Such magic powers unfold, beneath his master hand.

From *Illustrations of The Scenery on the Line of the*
Whitby and Pickering Railway (London 1836).

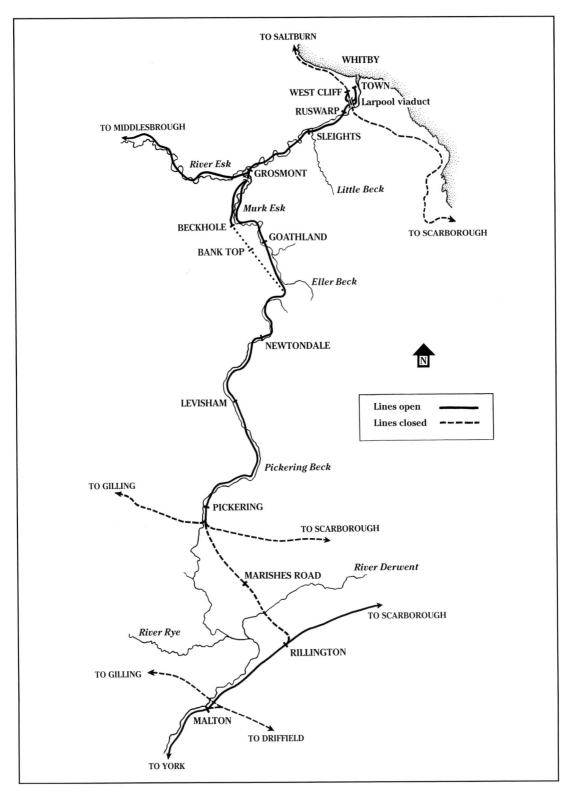

A map of the Whitby & Pickering Railway and associated railway lines in North Yorkshire.

THE
NORTH YORKSHIRE
MOORS RAILWAY

· A PAST AND PRESENT COMPANION ·

A nostalgic trip along the former Whitby & Pickering Railway and through to Malton

John Hunt

· RAILWAY HERITAGE ·
from
The NOSTALGIA Collection

© John Hunt 2001

All rights reserved. No part of this publication may be reproduced, stored in a retrieval system or transmitted, in any form or by any means, electronic, mechanical, photocopying, recording or otherwise, without prior permission in writing from Past & Present Publishing Ltd.

First published in 2001
Reprinted 2003
Reprinted 2007

British Library Cataloguing in Publication Data

A catalogue record for this book is available from the British Library.

ISBN 978 1 85895 187 4

Past & Present Publishing Ltd
The Trundle
Ringstead Road
Great Addington
Kettering
Northants NN14 4BW

Tel/Fax: 01536 330588
email: sales@nostalgiacollection.com
Website: www.nostalgiacollection.com

Map drawn by Christina Siviter

Photographs credited F. M. Sutcliffe are by Frank Meadow Sutcliffe FRPS (1853-1941) and are copyright The Sutcliffe Gallery, Whitby YO21 3BA (Tel 01947 602239, website www.sutcliffe-gallery.co.uk), by agreement with Whitby Literary and Philosophical Society.

Printed and bound in the Czech Republic

Past and Present

A Past & Present book
from
The **NOSTALGIA** *Collection*

ACKNOWLEDGEMENTS

In preparing this book I am indebted to the North Yorkshire Moors Railway and its Archivist, Graham Reussner, for making available photographs and other artefacts pertaining to the line.

I should also like to thank The Sutcliffe Gallery, Whitby, for so kindly making available the renowned work of Frank Meadow Sutcliffe, the Beck Isle Museum, Pickering, for the work of Sidney Smith, the National Railway Museum for the pictures of C. M. Doncaster, and Alan Thompson, for the photographs of J. W. Armstrong, as well as the various other photographers who have all been individually credited, but in particular Alan Brown, John M. Boyes, John Mallon, David Sutcliffe, Doug Hardy, Neville Stead, Michael Mensing and Tony Ross, for readily agreeing to the use of their pictures or those in their collections. I am also indebted to Trevor Ermel of Monochrome, Newcastle, for doing such an excellent job in printing most of the 'present' pictures.

As a result of their contributions this book provides a most comprehensive and fascinating coverage of the railway line from Whitby to Malton, vividly illustrating not only the changes that have occurred in over a century of operation, but especially the significant alterations that have taken place in the preservation era.

BIBLIOGRAPHY

Bairstow, Martin *Railways around Whitby*, Volumes 1 and 2
Idle, David *North Yorkshire Moors Railway Stock Book*
Thompson, Alan R. and Groundwater, Ken *British Railways Past and Present No 14: Cleveland and North Yorkshire*

CONTENTS

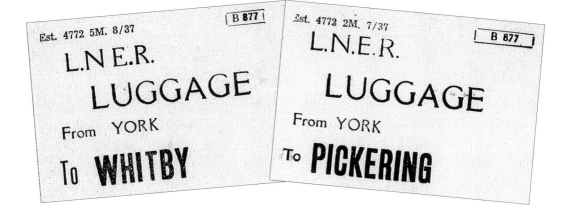

INTRODUCTION

The present-day North Yorkshire Moors Railway can trace its history back to 1826 when the suggestion of building a railway line from Whitby to Pickering was first mooted, but the idea really gathered momentum in 1831, culminating in an enthusiastic report by George Stephenson dated 5 July 1832. Such was the optimism generated that a meeting was held at the Angel Inn, Whitby, on 12 September when a share list was opened, and within a few weeks £30,000 had been subscribed. This confidence led to the obtaining of an Act of Parliament for the building of the railway, which was authorised on 6 May 1833.

A route was surveyed that would take the new railway from a terminus adjacent to the harbour at Whitby, along the valley of the River Esk as far as Grosmont, thence up the valley of the River Murk Esk to Beckhole, and a rope-worked incline to Goathland. The summit of the line was at Fen Bog, over 500 feet above sea level. The line then followed the valleys of Northdale and Newton Dale, glacial overflow channels up to 400 feet deep dating from the Ice Age, all the way to Pickering.

The first sod was cut on 10 September 1833 at Stone Quay, Whitby. Construction of the line to Grosmont involved no fewer than nine bridges over the Esk, and at Grosmont a tunnel, 120 yards long, 14 feet high and 10 feet wide. At the time it was intended that the line should be worked by horses. An outstanding feature of the line was the incline, 1,500 yards in length with a maximum gradient of 1 in 10, from Beckhole to Goathland. At Fen Bogs the ground conditions were such that it was necessary to sink piles into the 38-feet-deep bog and lay 'sheaves of heather bound in sheep skins, whole trees and hurdles covered with cut moss' in order to secure a firm foundation.

By 15 May 1835 it was possible to run trains as far as Grosmont, but the opening of the completed line took place on 26 May 1836, with the formalities commencing, appropriately, at the Angel Inn. On arrival at Pickering the celebrations continued in the Black Swan Inn; today plaques at both establishments commemorate this historical event.

However, the initial euphoria did not manifest itself in good fortune for the Whitby & Pickering Railway, and the horse-drawn railway was sold. Parliamentary approval was obtained on 30 June 1845 for the York & North Midland Railway to purchase the line for just £80,000 (£25,000 less than it cost to build it in the first place!) and to rebuild it for locomotive haulage. A year previously the Y&NMR had sought authorisation to build a line from York to Scarborough with a branch line to connect with the Whitby & Pickering. Stephenson had already surveyed two rail routes from Pickering to York, one via Easingwold and the other via Malton, and on 7 July 1845 the line from Rillington Junction to Pickering was opened.

The conversion works involved doubling the track, rebuilding bridges and the construction of a much larger tunnel at Grosmont. These works were completed by 1 July 1847, allowing the first steam-locomotive-hauled train to reach Whitby. However, trains were now more frequent, longer and heavier, and the Beckhole incline was proving to be an archaic bottleneck. Furthermore there were a number of accidents on the incline, culminating in two

In the 'past' view from the north end of the station platform at Goathland, J24 0-6-0 No 65678 storms into the station at the head of the Whitby-Malton goods on 1 August 1951. As can be seen, this was the top of a 1 in 49 climb, and many a fireman, even in preservation days, would be thankful for the easing of the gradient!

In the 'present' view, No 75029 brings the NYMR's prestige Sunday luncheon train 'The Moorlander' – the 12.50 off Grosmont – into the station on 25 February 2001. Apart from the singling of the track, the intervening 50 years have seen minimal changes. The gradient board is now on the opposite side of the track and latter-day safety requirements have dictated the rather unsympathetic wooden fencing. *D. Butterfield, N. Stead Collection/JH*

fatalities on 10 February 1864, but plans were already in hand to eliminate the use of the incline. The North Eastern Railway, which had been formed by an amalgamation of the Y&NMR and three other companies in 1854, had obtained an Act of Parliament on 11 July 1861 to build a new line to by-pass the incline. Known as the 'deviation', it cost £50,000 to build, was 4½ miles long, involved the construction of a new, double-track tunnel at Grosmont, nine bridges, and for 3 of its miles had a gradient of 1 in 49. It left the original line at Deviation Junction, just south of Grosmont, and rejoined it at Moor Gates between Goathland and Fen Bog. The new line opened on 1 July 1865.

Grosmont became a junction on 2 October 1865 when the line from Middlesbrough and Castleton was opened, and the increased traffic led to the enlargement and improvement of Whitby station. Ten years later Pickering also became a junction when, on 1 April 1875, the line from Pilmoor, Gilling and Kirkbymoorside was opened, followed by the line from Seamer to Pickering on 1 May 1882. Finally, Whitby too increased its importance with the opening of the coast lines to Loftus, Saltburn and Middlesbrough on 3 December 1883 and to Robin Hood's Bay and Scarborough on 16 July 1885. These latter lines ran to Whitby West Cliff station, and a single-line connection joined the two Whitby stations via Prospect Hill and Bog Hall Junctions. The Scarborough line involved the construction of the 120-feet-high, 12-arch Larpool viaduct over the River Esk.

Although the incline had been abandoned, the Beckhole branch saw a short revival at the start of the 20th century. A summer-only autocar and railcar service was introduced on 1 July 1908 from Whitby to a purpose-built platform at Beckhole. However, on the outbreak of war in 1914 the service was discontinued, but the branch remained open for occasional goods traffic to serve the hamlets of Esk Valley and Beckhole until a road was constructed to the former in 1951.

This was not the first closure, and the 1950s were to see a savage pruning of the railway lines of North Yorkshire. First to go was the Pickering to Seamer passenger service, withdrawn on 5 June 1950, followed soon after by the last passenger train between Pickering, Kirkbymoorside, Gilling and York on 31 January 1953. The closures continued with Whitby to Loftus on 5 May 1958. In an effort to make the remaining lines more economical, diesel multiple units were introduced in 1958 and 1959, and both Whitby and Pickering sheds were closed on 6 April 1959. The biggest blow came, however, with the publication of the Beeching Report in March 1963, which advocated closure of all the remaining lines to Whitby. Closure notices appeared in February 1964 and, despite strong local opposition, the Government's decision came on 11 September 1964 announcing the closure of the lines from Whitby to Scarborough, and Grosmont to Rillington Junction. The final day was 6 March 1965, when the DMU service was augmented by the steam-hauled 'Whitby Moors' special headed by No 3442 *The Great Marquess* and No 62005, which ran from Scarborough to Malton via Whitby. Thenceforward just the line to Middlesbrough via Castleton and Battersby remained open.

However, closure of the Pickering line had galvanised local people into action, and on 3 June 1967 the North Yorkshire Moors Railway Preservation Society was formed with the aim of re-opening the line from Grosmont to Pickering. A Company was later formed, but during 1968 it became apparent that acquisition of the whole line was going to cost around £100,000, well outwith the reach of the Company. Nevertheless, after protracted negotiations with British Railways a more realistic purchase price of £40,000 was agreed. This comprised 5½ miles of single track and railway property from Grosmont to Eller Beck, the summit of the line near Fen Bogs. A further £2,500 was agreed for the remaining 12½ miles of trackbed from Eller Beck to Pickering. The deal also included passing loops, six cottages at Grosmont tunnel, two at Levisham, three at Farwath, and the stations at Grosmont (up platform only), Goathland and Levisham.

Support for the fledgling revival scheme grew, and on 2 February 1969 the line's first steam locomotive, 0-4-0ST *Mirvale*, steamed from Pickering to Grosmont, followed two months later by two more steam locomotives, 0-4-0WT No 3 and 0-6-0ST *Salmon*. This acted as a catalyst and more rolling-stock arrived, including the first ex-BR locomotive, Q6 0-8-0 No 63395, in June 1970, together with two ex-Lambton Colliery 0-6-2Ts, Nos 5 and 29. Soon passenger services

This classic Sidney Smith picture depicts Pickering station, probably in the early 1900s judging by the total lack of motor vehicles. The view is looking down Park Street towards the castle. The level crossing is for Bridge Street, while the Market Place is off to the right. The picture is taken from the first floor of what is now the HSBC Bank, which was also used for the 'present' picture, taken on 17 April 2001. Insofar as the buildings are concerned there has been little change, but the motor car is now conspicuous by its presence and the station appears denuded without its overall roof, which was removed in 1953. *Sidney Smith, Beck Isle Museum/JH, courtesy of HSBC Bank*

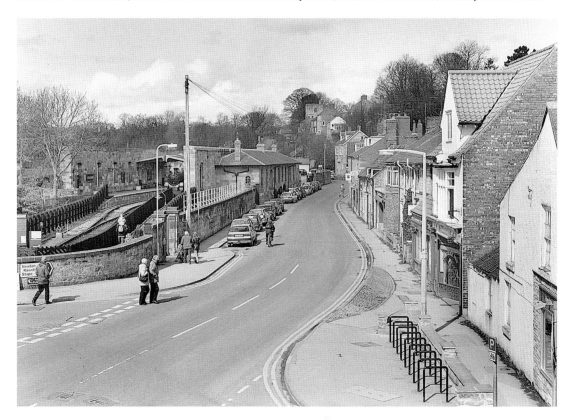

were operating between Grosmont, Goathland and a run-round loop at Eller Beck. During this time the North Yorkshire County Council took an increasing interest in the railway and agreed to purchase the remaining section of track to Pickering, and although one of the two tracks was lifted during the summer of 1969, the other was fortunately left in situ by BR in the light of these developments. A Light Railway Order was sought in January 1972, and on 1 May 1973 the North Yorkshire Moors Railway was formally re-opened by the Duchess of Kent. Although the re-opening train, headed by No 29 and NER P3 No 2392 was allowed to run into the station at Pickering, regular services beyond Goathland were operated by a DMU to a temporary platform at High Mill, Pickering, pending the resolution of problems of access to Pickering station. Eventually these were successfully overcome to allow the resumption of a through service over the whole length of the line from 24 May 1975.

Since then the NYMR has consolidated its position and become one of the top tourist attractions in the North of England. In 1986 it celebrated the 150th anniversary of the Whitby & Pickering Railway by running steam through to Whitby, and in 1998 celebrated its Silver Jubilee. Such has been its success that in the year 2000 it carried over 270,000 passengers and its turnover topped £3 million.

While the Whitby-Malton line was predominantly operated by locomotives of NER or LNER design, the A8s and J25s being a distant memory, today's railway sees a fascinating mixture of Class 142, 144 and 156 diesel multiple units on the Whitby-Middlesbrough line and 155, 156 and 158 DMUs and occasional locomotive-hauled excursions on the York-Scarborough line, while on the NYMR itself no one could have foreseen the variety of motive power that now graces its tracks. The 'Big Four' are represented and passengers can expect to be hauled by anything from the LHJC 0-6-2T No 29 to one of Gresley's legendary A4 'Pacifics'.

The NYMR had its beginnings in the first half of the 19th century; now, at the start of the 21st century, there is talk of connecting Pickering to Malton just as Stephenson did 160 years ago. In the intervening period there have been many changes to the railway, not least during the preservation era. This book attempts to illustrate just a few of those changes.

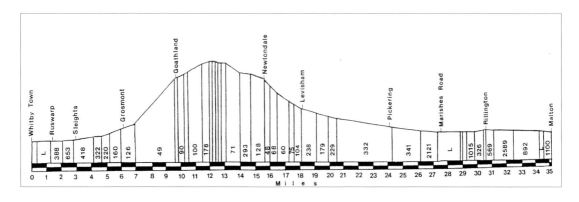

Gradient profile, Whitby Town to Malton

Whitby

Whitby station was designed by architect George T. Andrews, protégé of the 'Railway King' George Hudson and responsible for noteworthy architecture on the York & North Midland Railway and the North Eastern Railway, much of which survives to this day. The curved train shed, opened in 1847, once supported an overall roof, but this was dismantled in 1953. However, the stone porticos on the north (seen here) and east elevations have survived. The 'past' picture is the work of the noted Whitby photographer Frank Meadow Sutcliffe, and was probably taken in the 1870s. The present picture was taken on 8 March 2001. *F. M. Sutcliffe/JH*

The view from platform 1 of Whitby station; in the upper picture LNER K4 Class 2-6-0 No 3442 *The Great Marquess* awaits departure with a BBC filming special returning to York on 13 April 1964, while a new Metro-Cammell DMU departs from platform 2 on an afternoon train for Middlesbrough via the Esk Valley. On the right are platforms 3 and 4.

Today only platform 1 remains in use. The centre road and the track in platform 2 have been lifted and platforms 3 and 4 have disappeared beneath a Co-op supermarket. DMU No 142019 departs on the 12.34 to Middlesbrough on 17 March 2001. *Gavin Morrison/JH*

From Windsor Terrace, running alongside the western side of the station, countless pictures have been taken across the platforms with Whitby Abbey on the horizon. Class A8 No 69865, probably on station pilot duty, stands in platform 3 in the mid-1950s. On the right is Whitby Town signal box, which controlled the approach to the station; adjacent to it is the goods shed, which used to be a much larger building but was partially demolished by a bomb explosion during the war.

Rationalisation of the station layout and singling of the line from Whitby to Sleights meant closure of the box on 30 September 1984. However, it remained for a few more years until it was demolished around 1990, when parts were acquired by the North Yorkshire Moors Railway for use in the construction of a new signal box at Grosmont. The wooden building next to it was also obtained by the NYMR and is now on Pickering station. The 'present' picture shows the site on 21 April 2001 as No 142074 departs on the 12.34 to Middlesbrough. *J. W. Armstrong/JH*

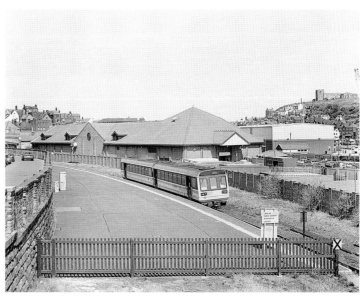

A busy scene on 23 July 1958 as a Metro-Cammell DMU leaves on the 4.30pm Middlesbrough-Scarborough, while B1 4-6-0 No 61071 waits with the 6.10pm to York, and L1 No 67754 on the 6.00pm to Middlesbrough.

On 21 April 2001 No 142074 arrives with the 14.05 service from Middlesbrough and graphically illustrates the severe rationalisation that has taken place at Whitby station, with just one platform in use and the supermarket occupying the site of the bay platforms and the goods yard. The station became unstaffed from 10 September 1988, a far cry from 1965 when Whitby had a staff of 46, including 11 drivers. *Michael Mensing/JH*

Just off the end of the station platform was the two-road Whitby locomotive shed, which dated from 1868, when it replaced the Y&NMR shed of 1847. In the first picture we see a busy scene outside the shed in August 1953 with a selection of locomotives synonymous with the Whitby lines, including three A8s, a J25, two L1s and two B1s. Identifiable are Nos 61030 *Nyala*, 67656, 69890 and 69888.

Although the shed was closed on 6 April 1958, it was not demolished but was used by various industrial and commercial concerns. On 28 June 1975 the track layout has been greatly simplified as preserved K1 No 2005 shunts empty stock into the station.

The shed, however, is a listed building, and in April 2001 there were plans to refurbish it as a heritage visitor, arts and education centre. The 'present' picture shows the site on 8 January 2001. *Kenneth Field, Rail Archive Stephenson Collection/JH (2)*

This was the scene outside the shed some time in the 1930s, as LNER G5 0-4-4T No 1319 and a Hull & Barnsley J23 0-6-0 await their next turns of duty. The picture will have been taken prior to 1938 since the last two J23s had been withdrawn from Whitby by that time. The second picture shows the same scene on 13 January 2001. *N. Stead Collection/JH*

Adjacent to Bog Hall signal box a public footpath crosses the line, and from this vantage point the upper picture of 1907 shows the busy loco shed to the left and the goods yard and carriage sidings to the right, with the double track in the middle. Note that the shed is so full that locomotives are stabled on the right-hand side of the running line as well. On the shed, coaling was by means of a hand-operated crane.

Today only the single running line remains into the station, with a run-round loop on the right controlled from a simple ground frame released by the single line token. *R. S. Carpenter, NYMR Collection/JH*

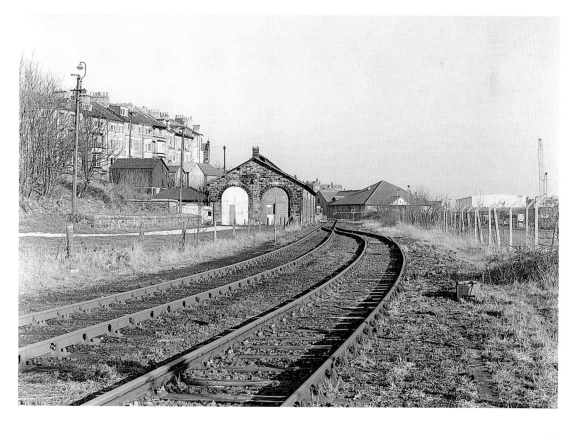

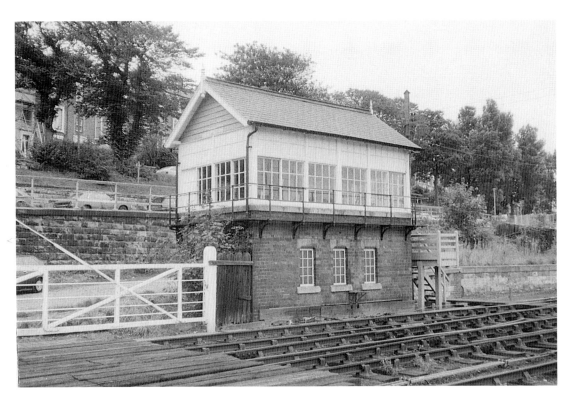

This is Bog Hall signal box while still in use prior to 1984. It used to control the junction of the single-track spur that connected Whitby Town and Whitby West Cliff stations, which ran beneath Larpool viaduct and joined the line from Scarborough at Prospect Hill Junction. The 'present' picture shows the same location on 13 January 2001; one of the mature trees has been felled, but the others are unmistakable. *NYMR Collection/JH*

A Whitby to Malton passenger train passes Bog Hall signal box behind BR Standard 2-6-2T No 82028. Dominating the town is the ruined abbey dating from 657AD and the nearby St Mary's Church, from which there are splendid views over the harbour and the coastline up to Sandsend and its fine sandy beaches. To reach the abbey is a flight of 199 steps, the 'Church Stairs', but the energy expended in surmounting them is well worth the effort.

In the present-day scene No 156443 on the 12.41 Whitby to Middlesbrough passes the same spot on 13 January 2001. *NYMR Collection/JH*

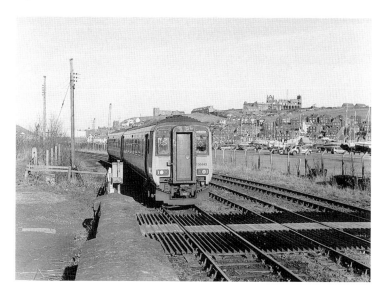

The turntable was situated between the running line and the estuary on the opposite side from the loco shed. A 50-foot turntable was sited here in 1902, but replaced in 1912. The 60-foot version shown here was built by Cowans of Carlisle and installed in 1936. In this 1965 view B1 Class 4-6-0 No 61276 is about to be turned.

On 31 January 2001 only the hillside beyond and a glimpse of the running lines on the right give a clue to the location. *Doug Hardy/JH*

Following the closure of Whitby shed and the wholesale introduction of diesel multiple units, steam locomotives continued to work into Whitby on the pick-up freights and occasional excursions until closure of the Scarborough and Rillington Junction lines on 8 March 1965. There was then no justification for the retention of the turntable and it was cut up in 1966. The first view shows this work in progress on 12 August, while the second shows the scene on 31 January 2001. *Alan Brown/JH*

While the line to Grosmont, following the River Esk, is virtually level, the line from Bog Hall Junction to Prospect Hill Junction climbed steeply at 1 in 50. Some time in the late 1950s the difference in gradient is readily apparent as No 42084 joins the Esk Valley route at Bog Hall Junction with a train from Scarborough that has reversed at Whitby West Cliff station.

On 5 March 2001 the vegetation has obliterated almost all traces of the former junction, although part of the retaining wall separating the two routes can be seen in the left distance. *K. Hoole, N. Stead Collection/JH*

L1 Class 2-6-4T No 67765 of Middlesbrough shed has a good head of steam as it drifts down the 1 in 50 to Bog Hall Junction after passing beneath Larpool viaduct with a Saltburn-Whitby train in the 1950s.

Finding the same spot over 40 years later on 5 March 2001 proved to be a challenge. The trackbed is very heavily overgrown, but a sole electricity supply pole, which appeared to be in the same position, offered a clue! Although the viaduct remains, the gas works building to the bottom left in the 'past' picture has been demolished.
K. Hoole, N. Stead Collection/JH

Although not on the railway line from Whitby to Malton, the viaduct at Larpool is so impressive that it warrants inclusion. On a dull summer's day on 1 June 1958 the '281 Scenic' from Hull, consisting of splendidly uniform LNER vintage stock headed by A8 No 69861 and B1 No 61010 *Wildebeeste*, passes over the viaduct. The Esk Valley route can be glimpsed on the far side of the river through the second arch from the left.

In the 'present' view on 5 March 2001 tree growth has almost hidden the viaduct from view. However, after many years of being fenced off, and surviving the threat of demolition in 1989, since November 2000 the public can walk over the viaduct as part of the longer coastal footpath along the Scarborough-Whitby railway line.
K. Hoole, N. Stead Collection/JH

Over 30 years of tree growth has meant that the uncluttered vista of Larpool viaduct from the Whitby to Ruswarp road is now no more, as these two contrasting views show. In the earlier picture a BR Standard 2-6-4T crosses the viaduct on the 2.30pm Scarborough-Whitby train in August 1957. It will reverse at Whitby West Cliff, then re-appear on the connection at the extreme right of the picture, descending to join the Esk Valley line curving along the river bank. On 5 March 2001 it is almost impossible to see the viaduct. *A. M. Ross/JH*

Construction of Larpool viaduct commenced in October 1882 and the first train, a locomotive and two trucks, passed over the viaduct on 24 October 1884. Costing £40,000, it was 125 feet high, 900 feet long and 5 million bricks were used in its construction. While it was being built, renowned local photographer Frank Meadow Sutcliffe recorded its progress. Two of these scenes show the methods used in the 19th century, which would surely not receive the approval of today's safety experts!

In the 'present' picture, taken on 5 March 2001, the sheer size of the structure can be readily appreciated. The gate pillars at the entrance to the gas works siding can be seen in both 'past' and 'present' pictures. *F. M. Sutcliffe (2)/ JH*

Opposite Viewed from the top of the viaduct, No 42083, freshly coaled at Whitby shed, climbs up from Bog Hall Junction to Prospect Hill Junction with a Scarborough train in the 1950s. At West Cliff station the engine will run round its train, then cross the viaduct to continue its journey. Following the closure of West Cliff on 10 June 1961, this manoeuvre was carried out at Prospect Hill Junction instead. The double-track line to Grosmont is just visible on the right.

In the second picture there is no sign of the former railway line, and to the right the track has been singled. Although the Whitby-Scarborough line closed in 1965, the track from Bog Hall to Prospect Hill and over the viaduct as far as Hawsker was left in situ with the prospect of possible potash mining in the area. Hopes were, however, unfounded and the remaining track was lifted in 1973. *K. Hoole, NYMR Collection/JH*

BR Standard tank No 80120 takes the Scarborough line through the passing loop at Prospect Hill Junction with the 4.20pm Whitby Town-Scarborough train in August 1957. The train came up the 1 in 50 on the left to Whitby West Cliff, where the locomotive ran round its train. The line beyond West Cliff to Loftus closed to all traffic on 5 May 1958.

The signal box survived closure of the Scarborough line on 8 March 1965, but was destroyed by fire in July 1971. In 1989, the date of the second view, the trackbed of the Scarborough line was in use as a footpath. *Both A. M. Ross*

BR Standard No 80118 arrives at Ruswarp on 19 July 1957 with the 10.28am York-Whitby train. The signal box can just be glimpsed at the end of the platform on the left-hand side.

After singling of the line between Whitby and Sleights in 1984, the nearside track was removed and the platform demolished. The gates were replaced with lifting barriers two years later and the signal box demolished. In the 'present' picture, dated 21 April 2001, No 142074 arrives with the 10.30 Middlesbrough-Whitby service. The station house, a listed building, is similar to the one at Sleights, and the G. T. Andrews design incorporates Tudor arches to the windows, and the chimneys have a hint of Tudor design too; since April 2001 the building has been a tea room and offers bed and breakfast accommodation. *Michael Mensing/JH*

Class B1 No 61154 crosses the River Esk at Ruswarp with an afternoon Whitby-York stopping train in the 1950s. Note Larpool viaduct in the background, the splendid road coach and the public footpath over the bridge.

On 8 January 2001 No 156471 leaves Ruswarp with the 12.41 Whitby-Middlesbrough service. With the old up line removed, and the removal of the decking to the footbridge making photography somewhat precarious, it was not possible to exactly copy the 'past' picture, but the road bridge over the Esk is still there and Larpool viaduct can just be seen through the trees. *K. Hoole, N. Stead Collection/JH*

In the twilight of steam at Whitby the shed acquired five brand new BR Standard 2-6-4Ts from Brighton Works. One of these, No 80120, brings what is probably the 1.20pm Goathland-Whitby stopping train across Ruswarp bridge in August 1957.

Little has changed in the same view on 13 January 2001 as No 156443 approaches Ruswarp with the 10.30 Middlesbrough-Whitby service. Beyond the bridge the siding has long gone, but the house is still there, and the coniferous trees to the right of No 80120 have grown somewhat in the intervening period! *A. M. Ross/JH*

Opposite No 42084 arrives at Sleights with a train for Whitby some time in the 1950s. In contrast No 156471 arrives with the 10.30 Middlesbrough-Whitby service on 8 January 2001. Despite the 1984 singling and abandonment of the old down platform, the station still has a cared-for look. *P. Cookson, N. Stead Collection/JH*

Class B1 No 61038 *Blacktail* enters Sleights station with the Saturdays-only 2.10pm Whitby Town-Leeds train in August 1957. The goods yard is well used and the ex-GNR coach appears to be in Departmental use.

In connection with the Stockton & Darlington Railway 150th Anniversary celebrations at Shildon in 1975 a number of special steam-hauled trains were allowed both on the East Coast Main Line and on the Battersby Junction to Whitby line. The latter were worked by K1 2-6-0 No 2005, seen in the second picture en route from Whitby to Grosmont, where it was normally based, on 8 June 1975.

In the 'present' view No 156487 calls with the 10.30 Middlesbrough-Whitby service on 7 February 2001. The down-side waiting room is now at Grosmont. While the former down line has gone, as have the sidings in the goods yard following the withdrawal of pick-up freight services in 1983, the signal box, although disused since 1984, remains. *A. M. Ross/JH (2)*

Photographed from the road bridge illustrated on page 32, A8 No 69878 approaches Sleights with a train for Whitby in the 1950s. From the same viewpoint on 7 February 2001, No 156487 is seen forming the 10.30 Middlesbrough-Whitby service. *J. W. Armstrong/JH*

Grosmont

Grosmont was, and still is, the junction for the lines from Whitby to Battersby Junction and Pickering, although it has altered considerably, especially over the last three decades. In the first picture, taken from the top of the signal box steps, a Metro-Cammell diesel multiple unit enters Grosmont with the 3.58pm Whitby to York service on 20 February 1965.

In the second view, seen from the same viewpoint, NER P3 Class 0-6-0 No 2392 pilots former National Coal Board 0-6-2T No 29 on the Royal re-opening train on 1 May 1973, conveying the Duchess of Kent. No 2392, as BR J27 No 65894, may well have worked freight trains over the line from Malton when shedded at York. Saved by the North Eastern Locomotive Preservation Group in 1967, it was restored at the NCB workshops at Philadelphia, County Durham, the BR depot at Thornaby and ICI Billingham before moving to the NYMR in October 1971. No 29, built for the Lambton Hetton & Joicey Colliery, worked on the extensive colliery system at Philadelphia and over BR lines to Sunderland until 1969 before being acquired for preservation; a year later it entered traffic on the embryonic NYMR.

In the present-day picture No 29 brings empty stock into Grosmont station on 12 March 2001. The Battersby line has been slewed to the left and the NYMR platform extended in 1990 to accommodate ten-coach trains, with the connection to the Railtrack line moved to a point just before the overbridge. In this latest view tree growth has almost completely hidden the old brickworks. *Alan Brown/JH (2)*

Viewed from the northern end of the Battersby line platform, the driver of B1 No 61034 *Chiru* prepares to collect the single line token for the section to Glaisdale as the Whitby to Stockton via Picton train enters the station on 13 June 1954, the last day of that particular service. No 61034 was a Stockton engine and replaced the more usual G5.

In the view taken on 10 January 2001 the tall bracket signal and brickworks chimney are long gone and only the stone wall on the left and the bottom of the platform ramp are recognisable from the 'past' picture as No 144021 enters with the 12.41 Whitby-Middlesbrough service. The footbridge was erected on 5 November 2000 to connect the car park on the old ironworks site to the station platforms; it came from Robertsbridge in East Sussex. *NYMR Collection/JH*

Arriving at platform 1 at Grosmont station in the 1950s is A8 No 69877 on a Whitby-Middlesbrough train. In the equivalent picture taken on 8 May 2000, No 144023 arrives with the 12.41 Whitby-Middlesbrough service. Gone are the signal box, signal, concrete lamp posts and loop, but remarkably little else has changed. One change for the good has been the provision of a North Eastern Region-type station nameboard and traditional platform seats in a partnership between the NYMR and the sadly now defunct Esk Valley Rail Partnership on behalf of Northern Spirit, operators of the Middlesbrough-Whitby passenger service. *N. Stead Collection/JH*

Opposite An unusual locomotive type on the Whitby lines was the Q6 0-8-0. Here No 63447 heads out of Grosmont with a Whitby-Middlesbrough freight in the 1950s. The siding on the left served the ironworks site, but was disused by this time. The two camping coaches can just be discerned to the left of the train behind the bushes.

In the 'present' picture No 144021 leaves Grosmont forming the 12.41 Whitby-Middlesbrough service on 10 January 2001. Although the loop and siding have gone and nature has encroached towards the running line, the bridge over the road and the houses leading up the steep main street of the village are still recognisable. *N. Stead Collection/JH*

This page The view southwards from a departing Whitby-bound train in 1963 shows the junction and signal box at Grosmont to good effect. Note the siding that served the goods yard in the apex of the platforms, and in which the two camping coaches were sited. From the re-introduction of camping coaches in 1952, two were located at Grosmont and one at Goathland, but they were withdrawn at the end of the 1964 season. They were painted in the green and cream livery of LNER tourist stock.

Following the singling of the Esk Valley line between Sleights and Grosmont in 1972, the signal box was closed, moved from its original site and stored for possible re-use; it was eventually acquired by the South Tynedale Railway at Alston. The 'present' view is actually taken from the same spot by virtue of the fact that in 1988 the NYMR tracks were slewed to the left and the remaining Esk Valley line track slewed to the right in order to accommodate the northwards extension of the NYMR's platform 2, which took place in 1990. The goods yard, devoid of track, is now the station car park. Often full, the overflow car park is on the old ironworks site, which, since November 2000, is now directly connected to the station via the new footbridge. *G. H. Platt/JH*

Right The track and signalling diagram for Grosmont in BR days. *JH*

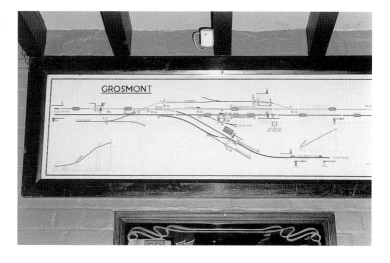

Opposite This classic illustration of Grosmont past depicts the ironworks at its zenith. The blast furnaces were in production between 1863 and 1891, and this scene was captured in about 1889. In the station a Fletcher locomotive is visible.

On 8 April 2001 the view from the garden of Rose Cottage is distinctly different. The blast furnaces have been replaced by the ubiquitous silver birch, such a characteristic feature of redundant railway or industrial land, and a National Park car park. The shelter on the Esk Valley line is still there, but additional buildings have appeared on the Pickering platform since the NYMR took over, including the 1913 wooden building previously on the down platform at Sleights, which is now the NYMR's booking office and waiting room. The locomotive is No 4277. Thanks are due to Mrs Christine for allowing access for this picture. *F. M. Sutcliffe/JH*

These three views of Grosmont station are looking southwards towards the level crossing and tunnel. The first shows the station in NER days, while the second depicts A8 No 69861 entering the station with an afternoon Malton-Whitby train in 1954. Rails lying in the 'six foot' and sleepers stacked on the left-hand platform suggest imminent track relaying. In the 'present' picture BR Standard 2-6-4T No 80135 enters the station with the 13.20 from Pickering on 15 February 2001.

In all three views the buildings are little changed, although in the most recent view it will be seen that the left-hand platform has had the wall removed and made into an 'island', while beyond the waiting shelter can be made out the new signal box commissioned in 1996 and utilising the 52-lever frame from Horden in County Durham. This replaced a small gate box, which can be seen on the gable wall of the Co-op building situated just beyond the level crossing on the right-hand side. *LGRP/J. W. Armstrong/JH*

A general view of Grosmont taken from the top of the tunnel, built in 1845. In the August 1939 view, taken just three days before the outbreak of the Second World War, A6 4-6-2T No 688 heads a morning Whitby-Leeds train that is being banked in readiness for the 3-mile climb to Goathland at 1 in 49.

In the summer of 1972 ex-NCB 0-6-2T No 5 heads out of the station with a short train for Goathland. Like No 29, No 5 came from the colliery system at Philadelphia, arriving on the NYMR in the autumn of 1971. In the station stands AC Cars four-wheeled railbus No W79978, the first item of rolling-stock to be delivered to the infant NYMR in 1968. *NYMR Collection/Andrew Beevers*

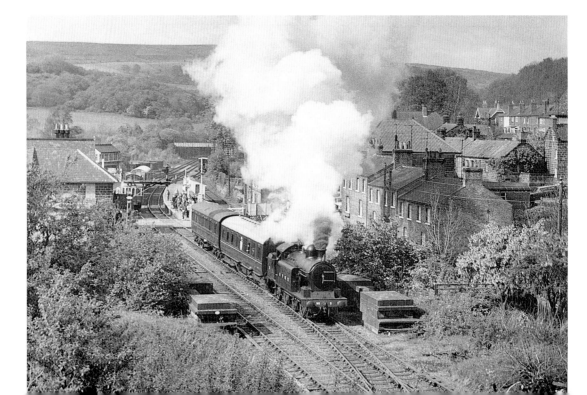

At Grosmont it was necessary to construct a tunnel through Lease Rigg and in doing so ironstone was discovered, thus giving rise to the local iron-making industry. This is the view at the south end of the 120-yard-long tunnel in NER days, showing the turntable on the right. Beyond, just to the right of the tunnel retaining wall, can be glimpsed part of the castellated entrance to Stephenson's original 1836 tunnel, through which horse-drawn trains initially ran. Through the tunnel can be made out the junction signal box.

In the 'present' picture, taken on 4 March 2001, the locomotive sheds and works of the NYMR now stand on the turntable site. When the preliminary works started in 1971 the foundations of the turntable were revealed.
K. Taylor Collection, NERA/JH

Viewed from the top of the tunnel retaining wall seen in the previous 'past' picture are the initial works to provide locomotive maintenance facilities for the fledgling NYMR. In a tradition that was to extend over a number of years, the Territorial Army provided week-long exercises on the railway, during which they undertook various projects. Here, on 13 May 1971, they are preparing the base for a locomotive inspection pit, as Q6 0-8-0 No 63395 comes down the hill from Goathland. Also purchased by the NELPG, the Q6 was acquired from Tyne Dock in April 1968, restored at Tyne Dock and then Thornaby depots, and delivered to the NYMR in June 1970. On the left are Tunnel Cottages; at that time they were occupied, but, faced with modernisation (they had outside toilets), they were demolished in 1989. Beyond them is Deviation signal box, which controlled the branch to Esk Valley and Beckhole, but which had been out of use since the branch was closed in 1951. It, too, was demolished, in 1977, to make way for Deviation loco shed, which is the most distant building in the 'present' picture taken on 22 April 2000. The buildings nearest the camera comprise the main workshops with the mechanical coaling plant beyond. *P. N. Trotter/ JH*

In the 'past' view, looking north towards the shed complex, the second siding into the shed, the frame of which was erected in 1972, is being laid by loco department volunteers during the summer of 1973. By now the cottages were being used by railway staff and volunteers.

In the 'present' picture, taken on 22 April 2000, the pointwork is almost lost in accumulated loco ash, and part of the 1972 shed building is visible to the right of the tunnel mouth; a locomotive tender frame sits on the pit illustrated opposite. Most of this building is now obscured by further additions to the shed facilities, including a fabrication shop (roads 2 and 3) erected in 1997 and, to the right of that, the running shed (roads 4 and 5), opened in 1990. In the right foreground is the framework of the coaling plant, while in front of the fabrication shop stands A4 'Pacific' No 60007 *Sir Nigel Gresley*, a regular performer on the NYMR between 1997 and 2001. *Both JH*

Another view of the shed area showing Tunnel Cottages and Deviation signal box in the 1950s. The box controlled the junction for the Beckhole branch, which finally closed on 18 September 1951, though latterly the box acted as a ground frame for the fortnightly branch train.

On 18 April 2000 the scene is totally transformed, with the main shed complex on the left, and NELPG's Deviation shed, erected in 1978, on the right. In between is the coaling plant commissioned in 1989 to replace various cruder methods of coaling steam locomotives and, at the time of publication, the only purpose-built such facility on Britain's private steam railways. The identical reference points in both pictures are several houses on the skyline. *K. Hoole, N. Stead Collection/JH*

B1 No 61084 accelerates away from Grosmont with an evening Whitby-Leeds train in the 1950s; to the rear of the train on the extreme left can be seen Deviation signal box.

In the early 1970s BR lifted the old up line, so NYMR trains now use the down line as far as Goathland, meaning that direct comparisons with 'past' pictures are more difficult to achieve. However, BR Standard Class 4 4-6-0 No 75029 *The Green Knight* is pictured in approximately the same location on 6 January 2001 hauling the 13.50 Grosmont-Pickering train. Acquired from BR in 1967 by artist David Shepherd, No 75029 had spells at Longmoor and the East Somerset Railway before moving to Grosmont in 1998 for overhaul. It entered NYMR service in May 2000. *C. Ord, NYMR Collection/JH*

Malton's ex-LMS 2-6-2T No 41247 pilots a B1 up the start of the 1 in 49 climb to Goathland at Esk Valley with a Whitby-York train on 10 August 1961. At exactly the same place No 75029 *The Green Knight* heads the 11.50 Grosmont-Pickering service on 5 January 2001. *Doug Hardy/JH*

Green End is a popular location for present-day photographers. In the first picture 1898-built Borrows 0-4-0WT No 3 pulls a Hull & Barnsley Railway coach to form the first passenger train up to Goathland on 27 April 1969. No 3 had arrived from Wallsend Slipway on the River Tyne on 28 March that year and was in the custody of the Newcastle University Railway Society. It left the railway on 26 May 1981 and is now on the Tanfield Railway.

On 2 April 1984 K1 Class 2-6-0 No 62005 heads a late-evening train from Grosmont to Goathland. No 62005 was donated to the NELPG in 1972, overhauled at Thornaby, and made its debut on the NYMR in June 1974. *J. M. Boyes/JH*

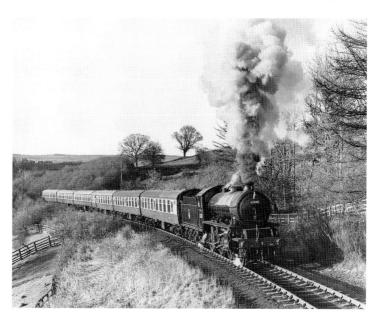

J27 No 65848 from Malton shed heads up the 1 in 49 at Beckhole with the Whitby-Malton pick-up goods in the late 1950s. At the same location classmate No 65894, as NER No 2392, heads the NELPG's 'The Silver Jubilee' special from Grosmont to Pickering on 26 October 1991. *C. Ord, NYMR Collection/JH*

Opposite The fireman has just put a round of coal on the fire as B1 No 61337 crosses the River Eller Beck at Water Ark on the climb to Goathland with the 8.55am Whitby-Malton train in the summer of 1964. Unusually, a public footpath also crosses the river beneath the railway bridge.

On 5 May 1971 No 5 works hard up the 1 in 49 with a Grosmont-Goathland train. *David Sutcliffe/ David Idle*

Below Beside the river is a stone inscribed in memory of a child who drowned at this spot. *Craig Donald*

From the path leading down to the footbridge there is a splendid view of trains climbing up to Goathland or descending to Grosmont. In the 'past' picture another B1 heads south with the 2.12pm Whitby-Leeds train in the summer of 1964, while on 5 July 1983 BR Western Region 'Warship' Class diesel-hydraulic D821 *Greyhound* descends the bank with the 12.20 Pickering-Grosmont service. From 1981 to 1991 the Diesel Traction Group had a number of its locomotives based on the NYMR. *David Sutcliffe/W. A. Sharman*

Opposite On 16th May 1961 we see No 82027 again, at the head of the 4.00pm from Malton to Whitby, drifting down the 1 in 49 at Darnholm just north of Goathland station.

The second picture shows visiting B1 No 61264 on the 14.20 Pickering-Grosmont on 19th April 2000, and in the final photograph No 80135 is at the head of the 13.20 Pickering-Grosmont on 23 December 2000. No 80135 was acquired from Barry scrapyard in 1972, returning to active duty in 1980 after overhaul at Grosmont. Ironically it carries the boiler from No 80116, one of the five Standard Class 4 tank engines allocated to Whitby shed between 1955 and 1958. Little has changed in the three pictures except for the removal of the former up line. *A. Robey/JH (2)*

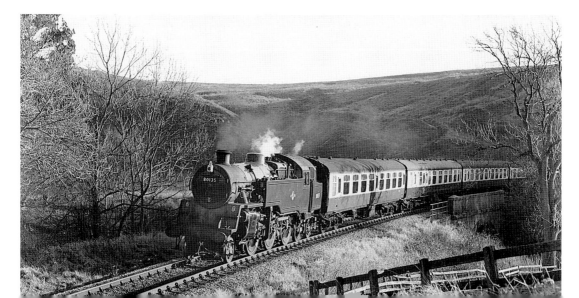

Another well-used vantage point to observe uphill trains is Darnholm, the area on the right being a popular picnic spot. In the 'past' picture an ex-LMS 2-6-0 heads the Whitby-Malton pick-up goods probably around 1963, while on 31 December 2000 No 75029 makes light work of the 11.50 Grosmont-Pickering train. *M. Dunnett/JH*

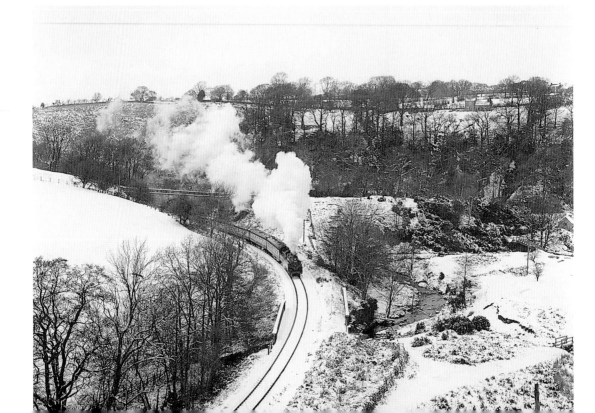

Goathland

At the top of the climb B1 No 61049 shuts off for the Goathland stop with a Whitby-Malton train on 15 May 1964, while in September 1984 the K1, masquerading as Fort William's No 62052, climbs the last few yards to the station with a Grosmont-Pickering train. *Doug Hardy/JH*

Goathland is a gem of a North Eastern Railway country station and has not only been preserved as such but developments over the last few years, such as the provision of a NER footbridge from Howden on North Tyneside in 1986, have enhanced its appearance so that it is now an award-winning station. Not surprisingly, it is popular for filming and has appeared as 'Aidensfield' in the TV series *Heartbeat* and as 'Hogsmeade' in the Harry Potter film. In the first picture LNER K4 2-6-0 No 3442 *The Great Marquess* has arrived in the station with a BBC filming special from York on 13 April 1964, while on 14 May 2000 No 29 pauses with a local train. *G. W. Morrison/David Idle*

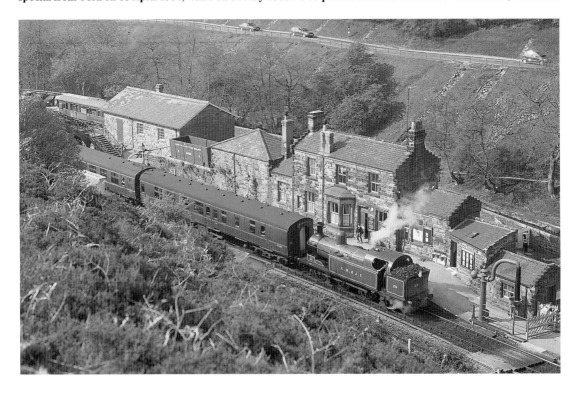

Two generations of railcar at Goathland: in the first picture LNER Sentinel steam railcar No 248 *Tantivy* awaits departure for Whitby in June 1937. These railcars were used by the LNER between 1927 and 1937 on Whitby-Goathland and Whitby-Malton trains. In 1935/6 there were three allocated to Whitby shed and one at Malton. On the right-hand side can be seen one of the camping coaches introduced by the LNER in 1933, a practice continued not only by BR from 1952 to 1964, but also by the NYMR. First available in 1998, the coach was so successful that a second was acquired in 2001 and was expected to be located at Levisham.

In the second picture the AC Cars railbus stands in the down platform while Andrew Barclay 0-6-0ST *Salmon* waits in the up platform to work a shuttle as far as the summit on 28 June 1970. The railbus, as No W79978, was the very first item of rolling-stock to be acquired by the infant NYMR, arriving at Grosmont on 9 August 1968, having travelled under its own power from Grangemouth in Scotland. *Salmon* arrived on the railway with No 3 on 28 March 1969. *T. E. Rounthwaite/JH*

The Cow Wath road overbridge at the south end of Goathland station has provided an ideal photographic vantage point for generations. The first picture shows the view prior to the bridge enlargement of 1908 (see overleaf), while the second depicts G6 0-4-4T No 87 on a Whitby-Goathland auto-train on 3 August 1925. In the third picture there is a poignant absence of any visible activity as a three-car DMU awaits a clear road for Grosmont some time in 1960. *G. W. J. Potter, Whitby Museum/K. L. Taylor, NERA/P. B. Booth, N. Stead Collection*

These further three pictures trace the development of Goathland since the NYMR took over. The first depicts the historic day when the NYMR's first steam locomotive, 0-4-0ST *Mirvale*, travelled under its own steam from Pickering to Grosmont on 2 February 1969. The second view typifies the embryonic days of the NYMR when the few locomotives were based at Goathland in the up sidings, and all but one of the line's locomotives are visible; from left to right, they are Q6 No 3395, *Salmon* and Nos 3 and 5 – missing is *Mirvale*. Twelve years later there is a much busier scene, as visiting 'Jubilee' Class 4-6-0 No 5690 *Leander* waits impatiently for the arrival of ex-NCB Austerity 0-6-0ST No 3180 *Antwerp* with a train from Pickering on 29 July 1983. *John Boyes/David Idle/JH*

At the south end of Goathland station the line crossed the Eller Beck for the fourth time since Grosmont. In 1908 the bridge was enlarged from two to three tracks. In the 'past' view the new bridge girders are being lowered into position on to the stone abutments, the left-hand one being clearly visible.

The second view shows the bridge as it appeared on 20 April 2001, with No 75014 on the 12.50 Grosmont-Pickering service. The water tower still stands and the two coaches, since removed, occupy the stone loading siding. However, all traces of the loading facility and the stone crusher that was served by the Silhowe tramway have disappeared. *National Railway Museum/JH*

Crossing the Eller Beck bridge two NER veterans are depicted, but 54 years apart! In the older view G5 0-4-4T No 384 heads south with a Whitby-Malton train in August 1938. On the right can be glimpsed the two six-wheeled camping coaches, and on the left the sleeper-built cattle dock, which was reconstructed on the same site and in the same style during July 2000 by the Cambridge OTC.

On 22nd May 1993 T3 0-8-0 No 901 takes a solitary brake-van to Pickering. Part of the National Collection, No 901 was placed in the care of the NELPG, which restored it to working order in 1991. *J. W. Armstrong/P. J. Robinson*

Opposite South of Goathland the gradients are easier and the countryside opens out to moorland. Near Saddler House, *Salmon* and its solitary coach climb from Goathland to the summit during a special gala event on 22 March 1970.

Beyond Goathland it was the former down line that was lifted, and 30 years later No 75029 *The Green Knight* passes the same tree with the 11.50 from Grosmont to Pickering on 6 January 2001. *J. M. Boyes/JH*

The summit of the line is 532 feet above sea level. Just before the summit there was a siding on the down side, which can be seen in the top picture, taken in the early 1960s, just beyond the milepost that records 19 miles from Rillington Junction. On the skyline to the left can just be made out construction works for the Fylingdales Early Warning Station.

The siding and signal box were still in use when photographed from a Malton-Whitby train on 20 February 1964, but by the time the third picture was taken from the 12.20 Pickering-Grosmont train on 2 January 2001 the box had gone, although the two huts flanking it have survived. In the distance the triangular radar building at Fylingdales replaced the famous giant 'golf balls' in the early 1990s. *J. F. Mallon Collection/Doug Hardy/JH*

Approaching the summit from Pickering, a B1 heads the 4.08pm Malton-Whitby train in the autumn of 1961. Nearly 40 years later No 62005 is in the same location returning to Grosmont with the MPD's steam breakdown crane on 22 November 1999. Both pictures show trains on the only level stretch of track between Pickering and Grosmont, and were taken from close to the Lyke Wake Walk, a renowned public footpath that runs for over 40 miles across the North York Moors from Osmotherly in the west to near Robin Hood's Bay in the east. *David Sutcliffe/John Whiteley*

After breasting the summit, trains shut off steam for the descent of Northdale and Newtondale. In August 1961 Malton's No 65844 sweeps round the curves at Fen Bogs with what, judging by the consist, might be an engineer's train rather than the local pick-up goods. At the same location on 4 January 2001, No 75029 heads the 11.50 Grosmont-Pickering service. *N. Stead/JH*

Coming into the Fen Bogs curves, Northdale Scar forms a backdrop to a Sundays-only Selby-Whitby train headed by G5 No 67248 piloting an unusual visitor to the line, an ex-LMS 43XXX series 2-6-0.

Attempting to obtain an equivalent present-day picture proved almost impossible since NYMR trains now use the old up line, from the edge of which the 'past' picture was taken. To move further to the left was out of the question, not just because of the vegetation but also the fact that the water of Fen Bogs is over a foot deep at this point! However, this picture of No 65894 on a re-creation of the pick-up goods on 18 November 2000 will have to suffice. *K. Hoole, N. Stead Collection/JH*

A8 No 69886 pilots a B1 on the final stages of the long climb from Levisham with a Leeds-Whitby train in the 1950s, the rear of the train having just topped a section of 1 in 54. To the right of the A8 are the remains of one of the isolated lineside cottages between Pickering and Summit occupied by railway workers until the 1950s, and which were served by their own special train on Pickering market day.

On 13 May 2000 No 62005 is passing the same point with the 12.20 Pickering-Grosmont train. BR lifted the down line with its concrete sleepers, but under NYMR auspices the up line has since been relaid with flat-bottom rail and concrete sleepers. *K. Hoole, N. Stead Collection/JH*

At the end of the 1 in 54 section lies Bridge 20, seen in the first picture on 28 March 1969, the day that *Salmon* and No 3 made their epic journey from Pickering to Grosmont. This was the last of several stops en route to replenish the locomotive tanks from the moorland streams. Seven of the people shown here were members of either the Newcastle University Railway Society or NELPG.

On 7 May 2000 little has changed other than the lifting of the down line as GWR 2-8-0T No 4277 crosses Bridge 20 with a Pickering-Grosmont train. The milepost is 17¾ from Rillington Junction. *J. M. Boyes/JH*

At the top of Northdale, looking towards Bridge 20, a Metro-Cammell 101 Class DMU on hire from BR is seen working the 18.00 Pickering High Mill to Grosmont service on 26 May 1973. The NYMR then acquired two twin-car 128 Class Gloucester DMUs to work Goathland-Pickering services until access was gained to Pickering station in 1975.

On 7th May 2000 BR Standard Class 4 4-6-0 No 75014 drifts downhill with a Grosmont-Pickering train. No 75014 was rescued from Barry scrapyard in 1980 and restored between 1985 and 1994, when it entered NYMR traffic. *David Idle/JH*

In the heart of Northdale B1 No 61319 rounds the curves up to Carter's House with the 4.08pm from Malton to Whitby in the summer of 1964, conveying, at the front, two through coaches that had left London King's Cross at 11.30; the rear vehicle is a Thompson centre-lavatory composite coach.

In the 'present' picture sister B1 No 61264 heads a similar-length train forming the 14.20 Pickering-Grosmont service on 19 April 2000 in exactly the same location. *David Sutcliffe/JH*

The view southwards from a point near the rear of the train in the previous pictures showing the characteristic chaired bull-head rail sitting on wooden sleepers and resting on ash ballast.

In the 'present' picture, taken on 6 February 2001, recent relaying has transformed the track, which is now flat-bottom rail on concrete sleepers resting on stone ballast. In the distance is Yewtree Scar, and on the horizon to the left is Saltergate Brow. *J. F. Mallon Collection/JH*

At the same location in Northdale another B1 hurries the 4.08pm Malton-Whitby train, comprising three ex-King's Cross suburban coaches, northwards in the spring of 1963. In comparison is another view of No 62005 on its breakdown train in the same place. *David Sutcliffe/John Whiteley*

Entering Northdale an unidentified Standard Class 3 2-6-2T – probably No 82027 or 82029 from Malton – heads a Malton-Whitby train in the early 1960s. Forty years later, on 29 December 2000, No 80135 passes the same spot with a Pickering-Grosmont train. Afforestation is nothing new in Northdale and Newtondale, but plantations come and go as can be seen in the contrast between these two views. *M. Dunnett/JH*

Halfway between Levisham and the summit is milepost 16, which is just behind the photographer in these two views. In the first, Whitby shed's No 42083 pilots an unidentified B1 on a Leeds-Whitby train in the late 1950s, while on 14 May 2000 No 62005 passes the same point with the 10.20 Pickering-Grosmont train.

The 'past' picture only had 'Beckhole' written on the back, which it clearly was not. Some lengthy detective work, relying on the small piece of what appeared to be the start of a retaining wall on the right, and a set of old rail-motor run-off rails on the left, managed to locate the correct position, though some 'gardening' to expose one of the rails was necessary! *K. Hoole, N. Stead Collection/JH*

Newtondale signal box was surely one of the most remote locations in the British Isles. It was last used in the early 1930s, but remained switched out until about 1952. It then gradually fell into disrepair, such that it was controversially demolished in November 1994. It was photographed from the 2.20pm Malton-Whitby train on 20 February 1965, but by 22 April 2000 only the foundations remained when viewed from the 13.20 Pickering-Grosmont service headed by No 80135. *Alan Brown/JH*

No 42553 storms up the 1 in 49 in Newtondale with a Malton-Whitby train in the 1950s. The engine crew are both leaning out to observe the photographer, with the fireman no doubt secure in the knowledge that for the time being at least his hard work is done as the gradient changes to a less taxing 1 in 128.

The same gradient board marks the exact spot nearly 40 years later as No 62005 heads effortlessly up Newtondale with the 11.20 Pickering-Grosmont train on 23 April 2000. *C. Ord, NYMR Collection/JH*

The climb through lonely Newtondale is a memorable experience for the passenger and a stiff test for the smaller steam locomotives. Trains of more than seven coaches would almost inevitably be double-headed from Malton as a consequence. The double-headed combination seen here had problems of a different sort – No 3 and *Salmon* pause to have their tanks replenished from the Pickering Beck near milepost 14 en route from Pickering to Grosmont on 28 March 1969. At the same location No 4277 coasts downhill with a Grosmont-Pickering train on 7 May 2000. *John Boyes/JH*

A rare combination of two B1s, with No 61053 leading, heads a lengthy excursion for Whitby up the 1 in 60 at Yorfalls, just north of Levisham, in the 1950s. At the same location No 80135 heads the 11.20 Pickering-Grosmont on 25 April 2001. *C. Ord, NYMR Collection/JH*

Raindale Mill was engraved by G. Dodgson for his book *Illustrations of the Scenery on the Line of Whitby and Pickering Railway*, published in 1836, and shows Newtondale before the railway arrived. After the line was built, Raindale Siding was located here at Yorfalls for public deliveries as well as timber loading. An additional short spur was laid from the main siding to serve as a crane road. However, this had an unusual point arrangement in that there was no crossing 'nose' but a jumper rail instead. In the 'past' photograph this can clearly be seen in the bottom left of the picture as NER 1884-built 38 Class 4-4-0 No 664 of Malton shed drifts down to Levisham. The picture was probably taken in the early part of the 20th century since this particular locomotive was withdrawn in June 1920. There were 16 Class 38s designed by Alexander McDonnell, formerly of the Irish GS&WR. In the third picture, showing No 4277 on a Grosmont-Pickering train on 8 April 2001, there is no trace of the siding, although the outline of Gallock Hill and Yorfalls crossing remain as recognisable reference points in both pictures. *Photos G. W. J. Potter Collection, Whitby Museum/JH*

Leaving Levisham H&BR J23 No 2460 approaches Raindale Siding with a northbound passenger train, probably in 1935. The H&BR 0-6-0s were not particularly popular with Whitby enginemen and had disappeared by 1938.

On 24 April 2001 No 80135 passes the same footpath with the 10.20 Pickering-Grosmont train. *C. M. Doncaster, NRM/JH*

Levisham

Some time in the 1950s B1 No 61045 drifts into Levisham on a Whitby-York train; note the locals nonchalantly using the down line as a footpath!

At the same location, although the position of the signal has altered in the intervening years, No 75029 approaches Levisham on 18 February 2001 on the 11.50 Grosmont-Pickering service. The locomotive, like No 80135, carries a 50H shedplate; in BR days Whitby was classified as 50G, so it was logical that Grosmont depot should assume the next alphabetical suffix in the York Division! *C. Ord, NYMR Collection/JH*

Turning the camera through 180 degrees, trains leaving Levisham on the commencement of the almost unbroken 6-mile climb to the summit can be photographed. In 1935 a classic combination of A8 No 1330 piloting York shed's D49 4-4-0 No 336 *The Quorn* is heading a Sunday excursion to Whitby. The D49 was withdrawn in January 1961.

In the second picture No 2005 heads the 16.10 Pickering-Grosmont train on 30 August 1993. *C. M. Doncaster, NRM/Peter Robinson*

These two views from southbound trains entering Levisham station were taken from the 8.48am Whitby-Malton train headed by No 82026 on 17 August 1962, and from the 12.50 Grosmont-Pickering service headed by No 44767 on 22 April 2000. The Station House and Cottages are little altered, but the level crossing now has barriers and flashing lights, installed in 1977 to reflect its much greater usage as gateway to the Forest Drive. The PW huts have changed and the siding has disappeared. *Alan Brown/JH*

Levisham station lies 1½ miles from the settlement of the same name that it purported to serve, and 300 feet lower, hardly conducive to intending passengers. The valley-bottom location is well illustrated in these two views from Levisham Moor. In the first a tank locomotive, probably an A6, brings a Malton-Whitby goods train into the station some time in the early part of the 20th century, while in the 'present' equivalent No 75029 *The Green Knight* approaches with the 10.20 Pickering-Grosmont train on 21 April 2001, as No 44767 *George Stephenson* waits with the 09.50 Grosmont-Pickering. Tree growth around the station and Grove House now obscures much of the station detail. *Sidney Smith, Beck Isle Museum/JH*

Despite increased patronage, especially by walkers, the station at Levisham has changed very little over the years, and its short platforms can still only accommodate three coaches! There is a total absence of any activity in the 'past' picture, taken on 16 May 1961, but on 23 April 2000 the presence of passengers on both platforms suggests the imminent arrival of trains in both directions, which will pass here. The siding has altered, and has been extended to stable items of preserved rolling-stock. *A. Robey/JH*

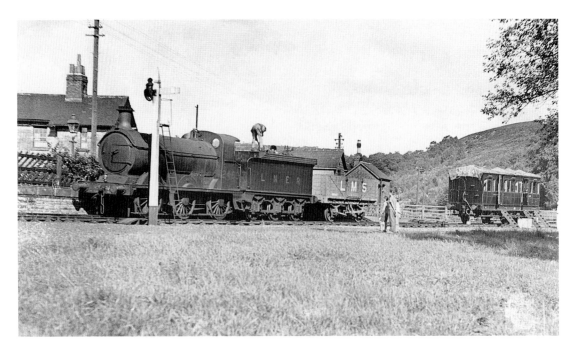

A timeless scene in the station yard at Levisham in about 1935 as J23 No 2469 handles a solitary LMS coal wagon, watched by a group of attentive holidaymakers presumably staying in the LNER six-wheeled camping coach on the right. These converted ex-GNR vehicles were introduced from 1933, and this particular example appears to have a leaking roof, judging by the tarpaulin!

The scene today is somewhat different with the extended siding used for wagon and coach storage and the rest of the old goods yard as a car park. The roofs of the signal box and Station House are still visible, however, on 3 April 2001. *C. M. Doncaster, NRM/JH*

This view of the goods yard was taken from a down train on 20 February 1965, just two weeks before closure. Thirty-five years later, on 28th March 2001, the view is much changed: the loop has been extended, as has the siding, which is full of vehicles, whilst afforestation has dramatically altered the far hillsides. *Alan Brown/JH*

In the upper picture D49 No 62731 *Selkirkshire* leaves Levisham with a Whitby-Malton train in the 1950s. Levisham was the end of the double-track section from Whitby and the start of the single line that extended as far as New Bridge, Pickering, the old up line having been lifted as part of the war effort in 1917. Legend has it that some of the track was destined for France but ended up at the bottom of the English Channel after the ship that was carrying it was sunk.

On 29th April 1984 K1 No 62005 makes a smoky departure for Pickering with a train from Grosmont. *C. Ord, N. Stead Collection/JH*

Much of Northdale and Newtondale is inaccessible by public road, and some sections have no footpath access either. One such stretch is between Levisham and New Bridge, where the line runs through the Blansby Park estates, owned by the Duchy of Lancaster. Between Farwath and Kingthorpe was Nettlebed Cottage, a gamekeeper's house situated next to the railway line and seen in the first picture in the first half of the 20th century. The house was demolished in about 1951, but the barn, to the right of the house, survived until December 2000, by which time it had become unsafe and had to be pulled down.

On 16 March 2001 the barn appears as a pile of stones to the left of the gatepost. Fireman Ian Pearson plays the role of the unknown fence-sitter in the 'past' picture! *Sidney Smith, Beck Isle Museum/JH*

Just south of Nettlebed Cottage is Kingthorpe curve, where B1 No 61276 is heading north with the 4.08pm Malton-Whitby train, conveying the two through coaches from King's Cross, in the summer of 1964.

On 19 April 2000 another B1, No 61264, accelerates off the 15mph speed restriction round the curves with the 14.20 Pickering-Grosmont service. *David Sutcliffe/JH*

In the last year of steam operation, on 20 February 1964, a B1 heads a Malton-Whitby train round Kingthorpe curve, while on 29 December 2000 No 80135 heads the 13.20 Pickering-Grosmont train in similarly wintry weather. *Doug Hardy/JH*

Old traditions are perpetuated at New Bridge signal box, on the outskirts of Pickering: in both pictures the fireman prepares to surrender the single line staff for the section from Levisham, and the signalman gets to work by car! On 17 August 1962 the locomotive is No 82026 on the 8.48am Whitby-York train, while on 23 April 2000 it is No 75014 on the 12.50 Grosmont-Pickering service. Note in the 'present' picture that the old down line has disappeared, as has the down loop and the siding into New Bridge Quarry, which remained open until 1 July 1966, thus post-dating the closure of the line from Grosmont by nearly 16 months. *Alan Brown/JH*

New Bridge crossing in the preservation era: in the first picture regular steam passenger services had yet to run as far as Pickering, but in this March 1974 view LMS 'Black Five' No 5428 *Eric Treacy* heads the BR weed-killing train. When it made its annual journey down the Esk Valley line from Middlesbrough to Whitby the opportunity

was taken to run it from Grosmont to Pickering and back, a practice that lasted for many years until 1990.

By 6 January 2001 the running line had been slewed to the old up formation, making a direct comparison impossible as No 75029 *The Green Knight* heads into Pickering on the 12.50 from Grosmont. Although Pickering station is signalled with colour lights, controlled from New Bridge, the up distant, inner and outer home signals are semaphores; the one seen here is the inner home. Behind the train, and above the tank wagons in the 'past' picture, is the NYMR's Permanent Way yard.
Both JH

In the first view of New Bridge level crossing and signal box, taken in August 1964, looking north, the quarry siding diverges to the left from the down loop, with the up and down running lines to the right. On 23 December 2000, only the up line remains. *Doug Hardy/JH*

The northern extent of Pickering station was marked by High Mill signal box, which controlled a level crossing, seen here as A8 No 69877 leaves Pickering with a Malton-Whitby train in the 1950s.

On 11 April 2000 K1 No 62005 leaves the station with the 12.20 to Grosmont. The level crossing, now automated, remains, and NYMR trains use the former down line, the up line and goods loop having been lifted. To the left, however, the old mill still stands. *N. Stead Collection/JH*

High Mill crossing has seen considerable change, the first picture showing the scene of dereliction in the years between closure and renaissance under the auspices of the NYMR. Photographed on 7 August 1969, the track in the foreground had already been traversed by *Mirvale*, *Salmon* and No 3 en route to Grosmont, but it was to be another six years before passenger trains would pass this spot.

On 22 April 2000 only the running line, the house on the right and the silver birch tree are recognisable from the earlier view. *Alan Brown/JH*

Pickering

The Rookers, an area of high ground to the west of the Pickering Beck, affords a panoramic view of the town of Pickering, with the spire of the church of St Peter and St Paul and the station prominent. In the earlier view, taken in LNER days, the overall roof is still in place and clerestory-roofed carriages are visible in the station yard.

On 10 April 2001 the scene is still dominated by the church spire and the station is still visible, although minus its roof. Tree growth, however, has obscured much of the railway interest. *Sidney Smith, Beck Isle Museum/JH*

Another prominent and historically important landmark is Pickering Castle. It dates from the 12th century and comprises a motte, built on the orders of William the Conqueror, and a Royal hunting lodge. Kings stayed here to enjoy the rich pickings from hunting on the Blansby estates. From the castle's Mill Tower there is a splendid view of the town, as well as the distant North York Moors and Yorkshire Wolds. The first view was taken in the early part of the 20th century and shows the G. T. Andrews station and its overall roof to good effect, as well as several prominent buildings in the town, including the Memorial Hall.

On 14 March 2001 No 29 is about to back on to its train in the station. Detailed examination of the two pictures will reveal that insofar as the buildings are concerned not a lot has changed in the more than 50 years that separate them. *Sidney Smith, Beck Isle Museum/JH*

The approach to the platforms at Pickering station is viewed from the 9.45am Whitby-Malton train headed by No 82027 on 17 August 1962. In the contrasting view from the same viewpoint on 22 April 2000, the train is the 12.50 Grosmont-Pickering service behind No 44767. Where the iron ore wagons stood is now the paint shop of the NYMR's Carriage & Wagon works, while the footbridge, which came from Walker Gate on Tyneside, was opened on 7 April 1997. Traditional LNER water columns now stand at the north ends of both platforms. Pickering station opened for regular NYMR services on 24 May 1975, and during the 1999/2000 winter underwent a major refurbishment. *Alan Brown/JH*

Photographed from the north end of the old down platform, No 5428 *Eric Treacy* has arrived with the BR weed-killing train on 6 May 1974. Lumley's mill and the Mill Tower of the castle are prominent in the background. The locomotive is standing on the bridge over the Pickering Beck.

On 18 April 2000 sister 'Black Five', the unique Stephenson link motion No 44767 *George Stephenson*, is running round its train. Tree growth and the carriage works hide the background, and a footpath from the station car park now occupies the open decking of the 'past' picture. *Both JH*

On 1 August 1949, looking northwards from the same bridge but on the opposite side of the line, G5 No 67273, on the 2.50pm from Scarborough via Thornton Dale, has just taken water.

Today the same viewpoint is compromised since the old up platform has been extended northwards, trees obscure the view of the mill, and the carriage works has taken the place of the water tower and sidings on the left. *Both T. J. Edgington*

Turning the camera through 180 degrees, the main station structure comes into view. In the first picture young passengers pose for the photographer outside the Andrews trainshed; Bridge Street signal box can be glimpsed at the far end.

In the second view, taken on a damp 29 January 1964, B1 No 61021 *Reitbok* pauses during shunting the pick-up goods.

Finally, RSH 0-4-0ST No 15 shunts stock in the station in readiness for filming by Yorkshire TV on 7 September 1973. No 15 was on the NYMR from June 1972 to January 1978. *NYMR Collection/Doug Hardy/ John Boyes*

Opposite The filming was for the serial *South Riding*, and the 'star of the show', the J27 as NER P3 No 2392, is seen entering the station in front of the TV cameras on 7 September 1973.

On 11 April 2000 No 80135 enters the station with a train from Grosmont. The NYMR has benefited from considerable TV and film exposure, latterly including the *Heartbeat* series, and various feature films such as *Possession* and the first Harry Potter film. *John Boyes/JH*

The south end of the station has often been photographed over the years; in the first of these three pictures A8 No 69865 has stopped with its Whitby-Malton train some time in the early 1950s – the bunting and Union Jack suggest that it could be the Coronation year of 1953.

In the second view another early excursion down the line is featured, as No 5 pulls a two-coach train conveying the Chairman and members of the North Riding County Council over the entire length of the line on 23 July 1971 in an effort to encourage support for the embryonic venture to re-open the whole 18-mile railway.

In the third photograph, that aim achieved, No 44767 *George Stephenson* has arrived at journey's end with the prestige 'Moorlander' Sunday luncheon train on 23 April 2000. *W. A. Camwell, NYMR Collection/David Idle/JH*

Opposite At the south end of the station there was a level crossing over Bridge Street. Viewed from the crossing on 7 August 1969, the station area is being taken over by nature. Today the level crossing is no more and a sturdy stone wall has taken the place of the gates across the railway. The former double track converges here into a headshunt capable of accommodating a locomotive for the purposes of running round its train for the return journey to Grosmont. SR 'Schools' Class 4-4-0 No 30926 *Repton* is embarking on this manoeuvre on 24 June 1996. No 30926 was withdrawn in 1963, overhauled at Eastleigh and sent to Steamtown in the USA. After 23 years it was repatriated, overhauled at Grosmont and entered service in 1990. *Both Alan Brown*

Looking south from the 2.20pm Malton-Whitby DMU standing in Pickering station on 20 February 1965, the level crossings in Bridge Street and Hungate can clearly be seen, as can Bridge Street signal box. On the right it appears that the relief signalman is making his way to the box.

In the 'present' picture, taken from No 80135 on 16 March 2001, the buffer-stop marks the present limit of NYMR operations. The loading dock has gone and the Midland Bank has changed its name. *Alan Brown/JH*

Opposite Bridge Street signal box is seen here on 7 August 1969, and its site on 19 April 2000. Note the cantilevered window to allow the signalman to see up Bridge Street before closing the gates to road traffic. Following demolition of the box it seems that the adjacent buildings have gained a new lease of life, although another casualty is the fine Yorkshire North Riding CC road sign. *Alan Brown/JH*

107

Looking southwards again, this is the view from the middle of the up main line on 7 August 1969, when Alan Brown recorded the sad remnants of the railway in a number of locations in Pickering.

Today, Bridge House, on the right, is in a much better state, and although the goods shed is long gone, the former retort and purifier house for the railway's gas works, which provided the gas for lighting the station, still stands; it is the building beyond the crane jib in the 'past' picture and behind the bus in the 'present' one, and currently houses a hairdresser. The other significant point of reference is the locomotive shed, the hipped roof of which can be seen to the right of the nearest telegraph pole in the 'past' picture and behind the lamp standard in the 'present'. *Alan Brown/JH*

Another view of the station by Sidney Smith, with the bank on the right and Bridge House on the left; Bridge Street signal box can be seen jutting out from behind the house, while in the up platform a southbound train appears ready for departure. To the left are the tracks leading into the goods yard; when shunting operations were taking place, it must have been quite frustrating for road users.

Today it is necessary to stand on the top of a high step-ladder to obtain the same viewpoint, and as the ladder was positioned at the entrance to a bus lay-by, the taking of the 'present' picture featuring No 29 on 14 March 2001 elicited some interesting comments from passers by! *Sidney Smith, Beck Isle Museum/JH*

The main Scarborough-Pickering-Thirsk road, the A170, runs right through the middle of Pickering, and it crossed the railway at Hungate level crossing, seen here on 7 August 1969 and the present-day location on 19 April 2000. The only recognisable feature in both pictures is the stone wall to the coal drops on the left. *Alan Brown/JH*

Just south of Hungate crossing, on the east side of the line, was the single-road locomotive shed, which housed locomotives out-stationed from Malton. Together with Whitby shed, it closed on 6 April 1959. In the 'past' picture, with the goods shed in the background, J25 No 65656 passes the shed with a lightweight goods train for Malton some time in the early 1950s.

On 14 January 2001 the bridge over the Pickering Beck still stands, now providing access to Taylor's joinery works, which still utilises the former locomotive shed. *J. W. Hague, N. Stead Collection/JH*

On the outskirts of Pickering the lines to Gilling, Rillington Junction and Seamer diverged at Mill Lane. On 31 January 1953 D49 No 62735 *Westmorland* is taking the Gilling line.

On 7 August 1969 the signal box is becoming derelict and it is only a matter of weeks before the rusty, weed-infested tracks will be lifted. In the distance can be seen Hungate signal box, the goods shed and the locomotive shed.

Finally, on 14 January 2001 the top of the locomotive shed roof can just be made out, but otherwise the scene is totally transformed. Residential development on the trackbed south of Mill Lane precludes an accurate 'present' picture featuring the crossing. *NYMR Collection/ Alan Brown/JH*

Opposite Looking south, this is Mill Lane with another D49 bringing what is probably a train of hoppers from the quarry at Thornton Dale past the 47-lever box and surrendering the single line staff to the signalman. The lines curving to the right go to Kirkbymoorside, Helmsley and Gilling. The actual junction of the Rillington Junction and Seamer lines was a couple of hundred yards further south, hidden behind the rear of the train.

In the 'present' picture the crossing cottage has new windows and has lost one of its Andrews chimneys, while the trackbed to the south is now part of a housing estate. *NYMR Collection/JH*

The Forge Valley line to Seamer is seen from the 2.20pm Malton-Whitby DMU on 20 February 1965. The through line closed to passenger traffic on 3 June 1950, but the section as far as Thornton Dale, using the right-hand of the two tracks, remained open until the final train ran on 25 January 1963. In the distance both lines crossed Haygate Lane, and the respective crossing cottages can be seen, the one on the right being identical to that at Mill Lane.

In the 'present' view, taken on 8 April 2001, there is no trace of either railway line, but the houses remain and, although extended, are still recognisable. *Alan Brown/JH*

The other main road route through Pickering is the Malton-Whitby A169 road, which crossed the Rillington Junction line at Black Bull. In the first picture K4 No 3442 *The Great Marquess* hurries its three-coach BBC filming special towards Pickering on 13 April 1964.

From the same viewpoint on 8 April 2001 there is little to remind the casual observer that there was ever a railway crossing here, except for the crossing cottage, of which the characteristic overhanging eaves and downcomer are common to both pictures. *Gavin Morrison/JH*

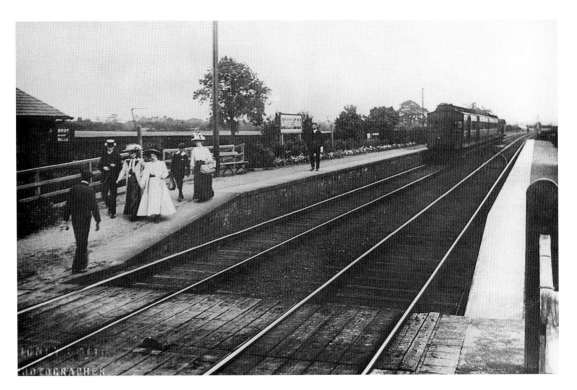

The only intermediate station between Pickering and Rillington Junction was at Marishes Road, serving a scattering of agricultural dwellings in this fertile area of the Vale of Pickering. In the 'past' picture a train of clerestory coaches departs towards Malton and a smartly dressed group of passengers makes its way off the platform, probably some time towards the end of the 19th century, possibly in 1881.

In the 'present' equivalent, taken on 15 January 2001, quite remarkably the station and crossing cottage, platforms and down-side waiting shelter all survive – waiting perhaps for the trains to return? *NYMR Collection/JH*

B1 No 61021 *Reitbok* of York shed brings the pick-up goods off the Whitby line at Rillington Junction on 27 April 1964. Note the bay platform, which only served the Whitby line, and the mineral wagon standing on the coal depot.

In the second picture No 156497 speeds past with the 16.48 Scarborough-Liverpool service on 3 March 2001, with only the brick wall to the former coal depot as a reminder of the former railway infrastructure. *Doug Hardy/JH*

It was originally intended that Rillington Junction would be the station for passengers to change to and from Whitby trains, but in practice Malton assumed this role and, together with other intermediate stations between Malton and Seamer, Rillington Junction was closed to passengers as early as 20 September 1930. It retained its G. T. Andrews trainshed roof for a further 20 years or so, as seen here in the early 1950s. The junction can be seen beyond the platforms.

On 5 March 2001 only the station house, much altered, remains, and the level crossing has been automated.
K. Hoole, N. Stead Collection/JH

Before the crossing was automated it was controlled from the adjacent signal box seen in his view of B1 No 61289 on a train from Scarborough, which, composed of LMS-design stock, was probably destined for the LM Region some time in the early 1960s. The earlier signal box was at the eastern end of the station.

On 10 April 2001 No 158904 forms the 17.54 Scarborough-Blackpool North train, with modern relay boxes having replaced the signal box. *D. P. Leckonby, N. Stead Collection/JH*

Malton

Approaching Malton the Scarborough line ran beneath the Gilling-Scarborough Road Junction-Driffield line. No 77012 heads the 11.00am Malton-Whitby train on 26 August 1958, while DMU No 155342 passes the same spot forming the 05.50 Blackpool North-Scarborough service on 13 March 2001. Although the Driffield line closed in 1958, the section of the Gilling line from Amotherby to Scarborough Road Junction at Norton did not close until 16 October 1964, and the left-hand abutment of the bridge over the main line and one of the piers of the bridge over the River Derwent survive. *P. Cookson/JH*

At the eastern approach to Malton station was Malton East signal box, which also controlled a very busy level crossing. J27 No 65849 drifts into the up goods loop with the returning pick-up goods from Whitby on 26 August 1958.

On 5 March 2001 No 158777 passes the same spot with the 15.52 Scarborough-Blackpool North service. Although the loop and sidings have gone, as have the footbridge and the tall chimney, the signal box and the far fence remain. *P. Cookson/JH*

Passing through Malton station is ex-LMS 2-6-0 No 43077 on a pick-up goods train, destined for Scarborough rather than Whitby, also on 26 August 1958.

From the same viewpoint No 158812 leaves the station with the 07.47 Blackpool North-Scarborough service on 6 March 2001. The two trains are using the same track, and the old up loop exists as a truncated siding on the left. The island platform has gone and up trains now use the crossover seen beyond the buffer stop to gain access to the sole remaining platform. *P. Cookson, N. Stead Collection/JH*

Viewed from the main platform, No 61018 *Gnu* stands in the up goods loop with a short mixed freight on 18 March 1964. On 11 December 2000 No 158775 heads west on what was the old up line. As it is on a crew training run it does not need to call at the platform, making the comparison with the 'past' picture more appropriate. Although the goods yard is overgrown, the row of terraced houses on the right remains unchanged. *Doug Hardy/JH*

This is Malton station looking west. In the first picture York-shedded V2 2-6-2 No 60968 calls with an excursion for Scarborough some time in the late 1950s.

In the second view B1 No 61276 is waiting to depart from the bay platform with a train for Whitby on 18 March 1964, with the typical overall roof and locomotive shed visible beyond.

Finally No 155343 calls with a Scarborough-Blackpool North service on 11 December 2000. Gone are the island platform, overall roof and locomotive shed. The station awning has been shortened and a supermarket now occupies the bay platform, sidings and goods yard. *NYMR Collection/ Doug Hardy/JH*

In this final look at the Whitby to Malton railway line, the first view is from the island platform with the signal box and locomotive shed to the left. The whole scene has a well-cared-for look about it, with a total absence of weeds and litter, and an interesting collection of platform paraphernalia on the right.

The second picture provides a closer look at the locomotive shed on 5 April 1958, with J39 0-6-0 No 64928, G5 0-4-4T No 67248 and J27 0-6-0 No 65827, complete with buffer-beam snowplough serving as a reminder of the inclement weather that could make operation of the line to Whitby quite difficult.

In the comparable scene on 13 March 2001, No 158775 recedes into the distance. *K. Hoole, N. Stead Collection/P. B. Booth, N. Stead Collection/JH*

MALTON AND WHITBY

Table 110

Station		WEEKDAYS									
							SO				X
		am	am	am	am	pm	pm	pm	pm	pm	pm
Leeds (City)	dep	3 0	......	......	9 10	......	*12 25*	1 50	......	4 25	......
York	„	4 35	...	...	10 15	...	*1 20*	3 10	...	5 10	...
MALTON	dep	**5 30**	......	......	**11 0**	......	***2 3***	**4 5**	......	**6 0**	......
Marishes Road	„	...	...	...	11 12	...	...	4 17	...	6 12	...
Pickering	„	6 0	......	......	11 19	......	*2 20*	4 25	......	6 19	......
Levisham	„	6 11	...	...	11 30	...	*2 31*	4 36	...	6 30	...
Goathland	„	6 28	8 25	......	11 47	......	*2 48*	4 53	......	6 47	......
Grosmont	„	6 36	8 32	9 7	11 54	2 5	*2 56*	5 0	5 10	6 54	7 58
Sleights	„	......	8 41	9 16	12 0	2 14	*3 5*	5 9	5 19	7 3	8 7
Ruswarp	„	...	8 46	9 21	12 8	2 19	*3 10*	5 14	5 24	7 8	8 13
WHITBY	arr	**6 50**	**8 50**	**9 25**	**12 13**	**2 23**	***3 14***	**5 18**	**5 28**	**7 12**	**8 18**

Station		WEEKDAYS										
						SO	X				X	
		am	am	am	am	am	noon	pm	pm	pm	pm	pm
WHITBY	dep	**6 45**	**7 7**	**7 50**	**9 40**	***11 50***	**12 0**	**3 30**	**3 40**	**5 42**	......	**6 45**
Ruswarp	„	6 50	7 12	7 55	9 45	*11 55*	12 5	3 35	3 45	5 47	...	6 51
Sleights	„	6 55	7 16	7 59	9 49	*11 59*	12 10	3 39	3 50	5 52	......	6 55
Grosmont	„	7 8	7 25	8 8	9 58	*12 8*	12 21	3 49	4 1	6 3	...	7 4
Goathland	„		7 35	8 18	10 8	*12 18*		3 59			......	7 14
Levisham	„	...	7 52		10 25	*12 35*	...	4 16	...	...	...	7 31
Pickering	„	......	8 4	......	10 46	*12 47*	......	4 30	......	......	7 25	7 45
Marishes Road	„	...	8 10	...	...	*12 53*	...	...	...	...	...	7 51
MALTON	arr	......	**8 21**	......	**11 1**	***1 4***	......	**4 45**	......	......	**7 45**	**8 2**
York	arr	...	9 9	...	11 50	*1 58*	...	5 38	...	...	...	9 7
Leeds (City)	„	......	9 55	......	12 35	*2 55*	......	6 35	......	......	......	10 23

A—For complete service between York and Pickering, see Sheet No. 30 SO—Saturdays only X—One class only

Full particulars of all L:N:E:R services can be obtained on request at stations

No. 29

Table 36

MALTON and WHITBY (TOWN)

Miles	Station	WEEKDAYS		Through Train—York to Whitby		Through Train—York to Whitby		Through Train—York (from Leeds on Saturdays) to Whitby			Through Train—York to Whitby		On Fridays 22nd July to 19th August, also every Saturday, is a through train York (dep 3.35 pm) to Whitby. On Fridays 22nd July to 19th August and Saturdays until 3rd September conveys through carriage—King's Cross (dep 11.28 am) (Table 35) to Whitby		Through Train—York to Whitby		Through Train—Selby (dep. 10.0 am) (Table 35) to Whitby	SUNDAYS	Through Train—Leeds to Whitby		
					T		SO											R			P
		am			am		am		am			pm		pm		pm		am		am	am
	35 Newcastle .. dep	2 11	....		7g30		8 0		8 35	....		11Ma26		1b30		3n30		7 10		7 10	....
	35 Darlington .. „	3 5	..		8j28		8 59		9 32	..		12M34		2b20		4n25		8 34		8 34	..
	35 Leeds (City) „	2 40	....		8 15		9 15		9A25	....		12H 50		2b40		4 30		9 15		9 52	....
	35 York .. „	4 30	..		9 25		9 55		10 28	..		1 45		3d20		5 35		10 20		10 40	11 15
					D T		D SO		W	D		D				D		D R		D	D P
		am	am		am		am		am	pm		pm		pm		pm		am		am	am
—	**MALTON** ...... dep	**5 20**	....		**9 55**		**10 24**		**11 0**	....		**2 15**		**4 8**		**6 4**		**10 50**		**11 10**	**11 50**
7½	Marishes Road .. „	..	..		..		..		11X12	..		..		4 20		6 16		..		..	..
11	Pickering .... „	5B44	....		10 16		10 41		11 21	....		2 32		4 28		6 23		11 8		11 29	12 7
17	Levisham .. .. „	5 55	..		..		..		11 32	..		2 43		4 39		6 34		..		11 40	..
25½	Goathland ...... „	6 12	8 15		10 44		....		11 49	1 30		3 0		4 56		6 51		11 36		11 58	12 35
29	Grosmont.. .. „	6 23	8 22		..		..		12 0	1 37		3 7		5 3		6 58		11 44		12 6	12 42
32¼	Sleights .... „	6 32	8 31		....		....		12 9	1 45		3 15		5 12		7 6		11 53		12 15	12 50
33¾	Ruswarp .. .. „	C	8 36		..		..		12 14	1 49		3 19		5 17		7 10		..		..	12 54
35¼	**WHITBY (Town)** arr	**6 39**	**8 40**		**11 5**		**11 27**		**12 18**	**1 52**		**3 22**		**5 21**		**7 13**		**12 0**		**12 24**	**12 57**

Miles	Station	Through Train—Whitby to York	WEEKDAYS		Through Train—Whitby to York		Extended to York on Fridays 22nd July to 19th August		Through Train to York Through Carriage—Whitby to King's Cross (arr 3.33 pm) (Table 35)		Through Train—Whitby to York		Through Train—Whitby to York			Through Train—Whitby to Leeds		Through Train—Whitby to York		Through Train—Whitby to York	Extended to York 11th July to 27th August		SUNDAYS	Through Train—Whitby to Selby (arr 9.2 pm) (Table 35)		Through Train—Whitby to Leeds	
			D			SO		SX		SO		K		D	D		D SO		D	T			D P		D R		D
			am	am		am		am		am		am		am	pm		pm		pm	pm		pm	am		pm		pm
—	**WHITBY (Town)** dep		**7 2**	**7 38**		**8 55**		**9 11**		**9 33**		**10 25**		**11 36**	**12 45**		**2 10**		**3 15**	**6 5**		**7 3**	**9 35**		**7 0**		**7 12**
1½	Ruswarp .. .. „		7 5	7 43		9 0		9 16		..		..		11 39	12 48		2 13		3 18			7 8	..		..		..
3	Sleights .... „		7 9	7 47		9 4		9 20		....		....		11 43	12 52		2 17		3 22			7 13	....		....		7 19
6¼	Grosmont.. .. „		7 17	7 56		9 13		9 29		9 48		10 39		11 51	1 0		2 25		3 30			7 22	9 50		..		7 28
9¾	Goathland ...... „		7 26	8 6		9 23		9 39		9 58		10 49		12 0	1 10		2 34		3 39			7 32	10 0		7 21		7 39
18¼	Levisham .. .. „		7 41			9 40		9 56		..		11 6		12 15			2 49		3 54			7 49	..		..		7 56
24¼	Pickering .. .. „		7 53	....		9 53		10 8		10 26		11 22		12 27	....		3 2		4 7			8 2	10 30		7 52		8 10
27¾	Marishes Road .. „		7 59	..		..		..		..		..		12 33	..		..		..			8 8	..		..		..
35¼	**MALTON** ...... arr		**8 10**	....		**10 10**		**10 23**		**10 43**		**11 37**		**12 44**	....		**3 18**		**4 22**	**7 12**		**8 22**	**10 47**		**8 9**		**8 26**
	35 York .. arr		8 40	..		10 40		11J12		11 20		12 7		1 14	..		3 47		4 51	7 45		9c 4	11 37		8 38		8 57
	35 Leeds (City) „		9 37	....		11 36		11 52		12 31		12 50		2t 6	....		4 23		5 42	8u50		10 8	12 37		....		9 42
	35 Darlington .. „		10F39	..		12 15		12 10		12f27		2 1		2t30	..		4 57		6 10	9h 9		10q 5	1 22		9 41		11 6
	35 Newcastle .. „		11F27	....		1 6		1 0		1e15		2 52		3t23	....		5 49		7k41	10h 2		11q 0	2 34		10 39		12a11

For other trains between Whitby (Town) and Grosmont, see Table 37.

D—Diesel Train.
A—On Saturdays departs Leeds 9.50 am.
B—Arrives Pickering 5.36 am.
C—Calls when required to set down.
F—On Mondays and Saturdays, also Fridays 8th July to 26th August, arrives Darlington 10.18 am, Newcastle 11.7 am.
H—On Saturdays departs Leeds 12.45 pm.
J—On Fridays 22nd July to 19th August arrives York 10.58 am.
K—Saturdays only. Runs 25th June to 3rd September.
M—On Saturdays departs Newcastle 11.5 am and Darlington 12.6 pm (Newcastle depart 11.30 am and Darlington 12.29 pm from 23rd July to 27th August).
P—Commences 1/th July.
R—Runs 10th July to 21st August,
S or SO—Saturdays only.
X or SX—Saturdays excepted.
T—Saturdays excepted. Runs 4th July to 26th August.
W—On Saturdays, also Mondays to Fridays until 1st July and commencing 29th August is Diesel Train.
a—am.
b—On Saturdays departs Newcastle 1.40 pm, Darlington 2.35 pm, Leeds (City) 2.30 pm.
c—From 11th July to 27th August arrives York 8.53 pm.
d—On Fridays 22nd July to 19th August also every Saturday departs York 3.35 pm.
e—On 18th June and commencing 27th August arrives Newcastle 2.28 pm.
f—Applies 25th June to 20th August.
g—Applies 18th July to 26th August.
h—Except 1st August passengers can arrive Darlington 8.46 and Newcastle 9.32 pm by Pullman Car train from York (Supplementary charges).
j—Applies 18th July to 26th August. On Monday 11th July departs Darlington 8.5 am.
k—On Saturdays arrives Newcastle 7.13 pm (7.24 pm on 18th June).
n—On Fridays departs Newcastle 3.40 pm and Darlington 4.35 pm. On Saturdays departs Newcastle 3.50 pm and Darlington 4.45 pm.
q—On Saturdays arrives Darlington 10.34 and Newcastle 11.35 pm
t—On Saturdays arrives Leeds 2.19, Darlington 2.36 and Newcastle 3.4 pm.
u—Applies 11th July to 19th August.

YORK, MALTON, WHITBY and SCARBOROUGH

Miles	Miles		WEEKDAYS															SUNDAYS		
			am			am	am		am	am		pm		pm	pm	pm	pm	am	pm	pm
		1 London (King's Cross) dep	11G50	....	....	4 0	....	....	9 0	9 20	....	11a 0	....	1 0	2 0	2 20	5 5	....	2 0	5 10
		1 Newcastle .. ,,	2 4	..	..	8 20	8m42	..	10 15	11 20	..	1 12	..	3 39	4 5	4 42	5 15	7 10	3 56	6 25
		29 Leeds (City) .... ,,	2 40	....	....	9 35	....	....	11n45	12p50	....	2 40	....	4 30	5 0	5 30	8 10	9 28	2 40	7 48
			am	am	am	am	am	pm	pm	pm	pm	pm	pm	pm	pm	pm	pm	am	pm	pm
—		**YORK** .. .. .. dep	**4 30**	..	..	**10 15**	**10 28**	..	**12 45**	**1 36**	..	**3 18**	..	**5 8**	**5 55**	**6 16**	**8 57**	**10 17**	**5 45**	**9 5**
21¼		**Malton** .... arr	**4 58**	....	....	**10 42**	**10 56**	....	**1 12**	**2 3**	....	**3 45**	....	**5 35**	**6 22**	**6 43**	**9 24**	**10 44**	**6 12**	**9 32**
	—	**MALTON** .. .. dep	..	**5 20**	..	Through Train—Leeds to Scarborough	**11 0**	..	..	Through Train—Leeds to Scarborough	**2 20**	Through Train—Leeds to Scarborough	**4 0**	Through Train—Leeds to Scarborough	**6 23**	Through Train—Leeds to Scarborough	Through Train—Leeds to Scarborough	Through Train—Leeds to Scarborough	..	..
	7½	Marishes Road .... ,,	....	....	....		....	....	....		....		4 12		6 35				....	....
	11	Pickering .. .. ,,	..	5D44	..		11 19	..	..		2 37		4 20		6 42				..	..
	17	Levisham .... ,,	....	5 55	....		11 30	....	....		2 48		4 31		6 53				....	....
	25½	Goathland .. .. ,,	..	6 12	8 20		11 47	1 20	..		3 5		4 48		7 10				..	..
	29	Grosmont .... ,,	....	6 23	8 27		11 54	1 27	....		3 12		4 55		7 19				....	....
	32¼	Sleights .. .. ,,	..	6 32	8 35		12 2	1 35	..		3 20		5 4		7 27				..	..
	33¾	Ruswarp .... ,,	....	C	8 39		12 6	1 39	....		3 24		5 9		7 31				....	....
	35¼	**WHITBY (Town)** arr	..	**6 39**	**8 42**		**12 9**	**1 42**	..		**3 27**		**5 13**		**7 34**				..	..
—		**Malton** .... dep	**5 3**	....	....	**10 45**	....	....	**1 14**	**2 5**	....	**3 46**	....	**5 36**	....	6 45	**9 25**	**10 46**	**6 14**	**9 33**
39¼		Seamer .. .. ,,	..	..	..	11 8	..	..	1 37	2 28	..	4 9	..	5 59	..	7 8	9 48	11N 9	6N37	9 56
42		**SCARBOROUGH (Central)** .. arr	**5 29**	....	....	**11 14**	....	....	**1 43**	**2 34**	....	**4 15**	....	**6 5**	....	7 14	**9 54**	**11d12**	**6d40**	**10 2**
		34 Whitby (Town) .. arr	..	..	..	12 51	..	..	..	3 50	..	5 27	..	..	..	8 56	..	..	..	..
51½		13 Filey .... ,,	7 40	....	....	11g46	....	....	....	2g57	....	4g57	....	6g16	....	7g31	....	....	6q50	....
64¾		13 Bridlington .. ,,	8 8	..	..	12g10	..	..	..	3g20	..	5g21	..	6g38	..	7g55	..	..	7q13	..

Miles	Miles		WEEKDAYS																	SUNDAYS		
					am			am		pm		pm	pm			pm		pm	am	am	pm
		13 Bridlington .. dep	....	....	6 58	....	....	9g24	....	11k45	....	2t21	....	....	....	4 33	....	6g49	9q25	11N17	6q36
		13 Filey .. ,,	..	..	7 24	..	..	9g45	..	12g11	..	2t44	..	..	..	5 1	..	6g16	9q50	11N41	7q 1
		34 Whitby (Town) ,,	....	....	....	....	....	8 57	....	11a22	....	....	2 18	....	....	....	....	6 0	....	....	....
			am	am	am	am	am	am	am	pm	pm	pm	pm	pm	pm	pm	pm	pm	am	pm	pm
—		**SCARBOROUGH (Central)** .. dep	**7 15**	..	**8 2**	..	..	**10 5**	..	**12 25**	..	**3 10**	**3 58**	..	**4 45**	**6 20**	..	**7 53**	**10 45**	**2 25**	**7 30**
2¾		Seamer .... ,,	7 21	....	....	....	....	10 12	....	12 32	....	3 17	4 5	....	....	....	....	8 2	10N52	..	7N37
20¾		**Malton** .. .. arr	**7 42**	..	**8 26**	..	..	**10 33**	..	**12 53**	..	**3 38**	**4 27**	..	**5 11**	**6 45**	..	**8 24**	**11 13**	**2 50**	**7 58**
	—	**WHITBY (Town)** ...... dep	Through Train—Scarborough to Leeds	**7 2**	Through Train—Scarborough to Leeds	**7 38**	**8 55**	Through Train—Scarborough to Leeds	**11 37**	....	**12 35**	Through Train—Scarborough to Leeds	Through Train—Scarborough to Leeds	**3 58**	Through Train—Scarborough to Leeds	Through Train—Scarborough to Leeds	**6 54**	....	....	Through Train—Scarborough to Leeds	Through Train—Scarborough to Leeds
	1½	Ruswarp .. ,,		7 5		7 41	9 0		11 40	..	12 38			4 1			7 0	..	..		
	3	Sleights .... ,,		7 9		7 45	9 4		11 44	....	12 42			4 5			7 5	....	....		
	6¼	Grosmont .. ,,		7 17		7 53	9 13		11 52	..	12 50			4 13			7 13	..	..		
	9¾	Goathland ...... ,,		7 26		8 2	9 23		12 1	....	12 59			4 22			7 23	....	....		
	18¼	Levisham .. .. ,,		7 41		—	9 40		12 16	..	—			4 37			7 40	..	..		
	24¼	Pickering ...... ,,		7 53		....	9 52		12 28	....	....			4 49			7 54	....	....		
	27¾	Marishes Road .. ,,		7 59		..	..		..	..	..			..			..	..	..		
	35¼	**Malton** .... arr		**8 10**		....	**10 7**		**12 43**	....	....			**5 4**			**8 9**	....	....		
—		**Malton** .. .. dep	**7 43**	**8 13**	**8 28**	..	..	**10 34**	..	**12 55**	..	**3 41**	**4 29**	**5 5**	**5 12**	**6 46**	..	**8 29**	**11 15**	**2 51**	**8 0**
42		**YORK** .... arr	**8 10**	**8 40**	**8 56**	....	....	**11 1**	....	**1 22**	....	**4 8**	**4 56**	**5 32**	**5 39**	**7 13**	....	**8 57**	**11 42**	**3 18**	**8 27**
67½		29 Leeds (City) .. arr	8 51	..	9 37	..	..	11h49	..	2 6	..	4 48	5 46	..	6 18	7 55	..	10 0	12 35	4 2	9 7
122½		1 Newcastle .... ,,	10 33	....	11 20	....	....	12 53	....	3 18	....	6 0	6 40	....	7 52	9j22	....	10A38	1 56	5 14	10 36
230		1 London (King's Cross) ,,	..	..	12 48	..	..	3 11	..	5 34	..	..	8 19	..	9e50	..	..	2f56	4 27	7 36	3 4

For other trains between Seamer and Scarborough, see Table 13.

For other trains between Whitby (Town) and Grosmont, see Table 34.

A—On Saturday night/Sunday mornings arrives Newcastle 12.39 am
C—Calls when required to set down.
D—Arrives Pickering 5.36 am.
G—pm. On Sunday nights departs King's Cross 11.45 pm.
N—Applies on 15th, 22nd, 29th September, 1963 and commencing 17th May, 1964.
a—am.
d—On 15th, 22nd, 29th September 1963 and commencing 17th May, 1964 arrives Scarborough 3 minutes later.
e—On Saturdays arrives King's Cross 10.6 pm.
f—On Sunday mornings arrives King's Cross 3.31 am.
g—Connection at Seamer.
h—On Saturdays arrives Leeds 11.53 am.
j—On Fridays arrives Newcastle 9.15 pm.
k—am. Connection at Seamer.
m—Except Saturdays and not on 25th, 26th December, 27th, 30th March and 18th May passengers can depart Newcastle 9.0 am by Pullman Car train (supplementary charge).
n—On Saturdays departs Leeds 11.15 am.
p—pm.
q—Applies on 15th, 22nd, 29th September, 1963 and commencing 17th May, 1964. Connection at Seamer.
t—Connection at Seamer. On Saturdays departs Bridlington 2g29 pm and Filey 2g53 pm.

Above left LNER, Winter 1942 *Left* BR, Summer 1960 *Above* BR, Winter 1963/4

Table 45 — Mondays to Saturdays

Whitby → Middlesbrough

Miles	Station	NS SO A	NS SO B	NS SX C	NS SX D	NS SX	NS SO	NS SO	NS SX	NS SO	NS SX	NS E	NS G	NS SO	NS SX	NS
0	Whitby d							08 45	08 52	12 34	12 41			15 47	16 05	19 13
1½	Ruswarp d							08 49	08 56	12 38	12 45			15 51	16 09	19 17
3	Sleights d							08 54	09 01	12 43	12 50			15 56	16 14	19 22
6½	Grosmont d							09 02	09 09	12 51	12 58			16 04	16 22	19 30
7½	Egton d							09 05	09 12	12 54	13 01			16 07	16 26	19 33
9½	Glaisdale a							09 09	09 16	12 58	13 05			16 11	16 30	19 37
—	d							09 12	09 19	13 01	13 08			16 14	16 33	19 40
11½	Lealholm d							09 17	09 24	13 06	13 13			16 19	16 38	19 45
15	Danby d							09 23	09 30	13 12	13 19			16 25	16 45	19 51
16½	Castleton Moor d							09 26	09 33	13 15	13 22			16 28	16 49	19 54
18½	Commondale d							09 30	09 37	13 19	13 26			16 32	16 52	19 58
22½	Kildale d							09 37	09 44	13 26	13 33			16 39	16 59	20 05
24	Battersby d							09 42	09 49	13 31	13 38			16 44	17 04	20 10
—	d							09 46	09 53	13 35	13 42			16 48	17 09	20 14
26½	Great Ayton d							09 51	09 58	13 40	13 47			16 53	17 14	20 19
30½	Nunthorpe d	07 32	07 32	07 32	07 32	08 33	08 34	09 58	10 05	13 47	13 54	16 30	16 31	17 00	17 21	20 26
31	Gypsy Lane d	07 34	07 34	07 34	07 34	08 35	08 36	10 00	10 07	13 49	13 56	16 32	16 35	17 02	17 23	20 28
32	Marton d	07 36	07 36	07 36	07 36	08 37	08 38	10 03	10 10	13 52	13 59	16 34	16 35	17 05	17 25	20 31
35	Middlesbrough a	07 43	07 43	07 43	07 43	08 43	08 44	10 11	10 18	14 40	14 41	16 40	16 41	17 14	17 34	20 39
—	Darlington 🚆 44 a	08 30	08 30	08 38	08 38	09 16	10 07	10 52	10 52	14 50	14 50	17 20	17 32	17 49	18 24	21b19
—	Newcastle 🚆 46 a	09 06	09 23	09 06	09 23	09e56	10e50	11c37	11c34	15c34	15c35	18c13	18t20	18c59	19a11	22g19

Sundays

Until 1 October, 3 to 17 December and from 11 March

Station	NS	NS	NS H	NS
Whitby d	12 20	13 03	16 05	17 15
Ruswarp d	12 24	13 07	16 09	17 19
Sleights d	12 29	13 12	16 14	17 24
Grosmont d	12 37	13 20	16 22	17 32
Egton d	12 40	13 23	16 25	17 35
Glaisdale a	12 44	13 27	16 29	17 39
d	12 47	13 30	16 32	17 42
Lealholm d	12 52	13 35	16 37	17 47
Danby d	12 58	13 41	16 43	17 53
Castleton Moor d	13 01	13 44	16 46	17 56
Commondale d	13 05	13 48	16 50	18 00
Kildale d	13 12	13 55	16 57	18 07
Battersby d	13 21	14 04	17 02	18 12
d			17 06	18 16
Great Ayton d	13 26	14 09	17 11	18 21
Nunthorpe d	13 33	14 16	17 18	18 28
Gypsy Lane d	13 35	14 18	17 20	18 30
Marton d	13 38	14 21	17 23	18 33
Middlesbrough a	13 46	14 29	17 33	18 43
Darlington 🚆 44 a			18 56	19 13
Newcastle 🚆 46 a				

For general notes see front of timetable

A Until 24 February and from 14 April.
B 3 March to 7 April. To Sunderland (Table 46).
C Until 23 February and from 9 April.
D 26 February to 6 April. To Sunderland (Table 46)
E 3 March to 7 April to Sunderland (Table 46)
G 26 February to 6 April to Sunderland (Table 46)
H To MetroCentre (Table 48). 11 March to 8 April to Sunderland (Table 46)
b Saturdays arr. 2127
c Change at Middlesbrough and Darlington
e 3 March to 7 April arr. 1051
f Until 23 February and from 9 April change at Middlesbrough. 26 February to 6 April change at Middlesbrough and Darlington
g Change at Middlesbrough and Darlington. Saturdays arr. 2211

> From time to time it is necessary to undertake extensive engineering work at weekends. This frequently affects services and passengers are advised to look for specific announcements of possible diversions and delays making a final check at stations or telephone enquiry bureaux

Arriva, Northern Spirit, Middlesbrough-Whitby, 2001

INDEX OF LOCATIONS